READING, *WRITING* and **ARITHM3TIC**

READING, *WRITING* and **ARITHM3TIC**

Mastering the Three Rs of an Old-Fashioned Education

DANIEL SMITH

Michael O'Mara Books Ltd

For Rosie (the best R of them all)

First published in Great Britain in 2013 by
Michael O'Mara Books Limited
9 Lion Yard
Tremadoc Road
London SW4 7NQ

A CIP catalogue record for this book is
available from the British Library.

Papers used by Michael O'Mara Books Limited are natural,
recyclable products made from wood grown in sustainable forests.
The manufacturing processes conform to the environmental
regulations of the country of origin.

ISBN: 978-1-78243-044-5 in hardback print format
ISBN: 978-1-78243-053-7 in ePub format
ISBN: 978-1-78243-054-4 in Mobipocket format

1 2 3 4 5 6 7 8 9 10

Lettering by Patrick Knowles
Typesetting designed by www.glensaville.com
Printed and bound by CPI Group (UK) Ltd, Croydon, CR0 4YY

www.mombooks.com

CONTENTS

INTRODUCTION

'Without education, we are in a horrible and deadly danger of taking educated people seriously.'

G.K. Chesterton

I'd like to begin today's lesson with a simple question: What are the Three Rs? Well, in short, the Three Rs comprise Reading, Writing and Arithmetic: the traditional foundation stones of a good, old-fashioned education. The joke is, of course, that the expression demonstrates scant regard for the niceties of spelling, but we'll just have to let that one slide.

Historians can't agree on the provenance of the term, but the consensus is 'the Three Rs' became common currency after a speech made in 1825 by Tory MP Sir William Curtis. A successful man of commerce – he was the son of a sea-biscuit manufacturer, hence the nickname Billy Biscuit – Curtis was one of the more colourful MPs of the Georgian age, known as much for his protuberant belly and bright red nose as for his predilection for catchphrases. One day, bored by a Commons debate on the importance of Classical Latin and Greek in the school curriculum, Curtis rose to his feet and announced to his fellow MPs: 'What children need is the Three Rs: Readin', Ritin' and Rithmatic.'

Whether Curtis used the expression for comic effect or out of genuine confusion isn't clear. He was, however, subject to widespread lampooning and became the frequent subject of satirical cartoons; but at the same time his comments ignited an enduring argument as to what should constitute a basic education.

The Three Rs still serve as a weapon with which rival politicians and other interested parties beat each other over the head. On one side of the debate are those who hunger for Curtis' system of yesteryear – a somewhat rose-tinted vision that demands rigorous testing of students' skills in the basics of English and maths. On the other side are those demanding an entire overhaul of this philosophy. In a 2012 article for the *Huffington Post*, clinical psychologist Ben Michaelis wrote in favour of spending less time and money on the Three Rs and more on the Three Cs – Creativity, Confidence and Character.

But of course the truth is that education is about more than simply learning tables of verbs by rote, or perfecting the loops and curves of beautiful handwriting. But it's equally true that this has always been the case. Historically, creativity, confidence and character have been nurtured in equal measure to reading, writing and arithmetic by a broad and liberal syllabus.

So, while this book isn't going to give you a complete education, it will offer you the opportunity to revisit – or, indeed, learn for the very first time – the fundamentals. And not only are the exercises contained lots of fun, they'll also give you a grounding in those most modern and relevant skills of communication, numeracy and logical thinking.

G.K. Chesterton once said education is 'simply the soul of a society as it passes from one generation to another'. It's also a gift that should be cherished, so enjoy this brief but, hopefully, illuminating journey through the magical worlds of language and number. And have your answers to the long division questions on my desk by Monday.

SECTION I
READING

Lots of us love to immerse ourselves in a good book, but do you ever find yourself forgetting what you've just read? Or taking an age to reach the end of the story? They're common afflictions, but the good news is there's help at hand. Covering the basics of speed-reading and comprehension, this section will turn you into a quick and perceptive reader before you can say 'please turn the page'.

SPEEDY GONZALES
SPEED-READING

On a basic level, reading is the process of decoding a series of symbols (letters, numbers and punctuation marks) in order to access their meaning. In a wider sense, reading opens up unlimited worlds to us, from taut psychological thrillers to histories of the world – it's wonderful to lose yourself in a great story.

Reading is a fundamental skill that most of us learn in childhood, and, rather unsurprisingly, we get more efficient at it the more we practise it. Studies suggest that the average adult reads between 175 and 350 words per minute. However, it's possible to develop skills to enable you to read even faster than this while still absorbing and understanding the words your eyes are scanning. *Speed-reading* is thus not only about reading quicker, but also reading better.

GETTING UP TO SPEED: MASTERING THE ART OF SPEED-READING

Here are some tips to help you improve your reading skills:

1. **Find an environment conducive to reading** – somewhere quiet and peaceful where you'll be able to concentrate.
2. **Read in chunks**. When we're first taught to read, we're encouraged (quite rightly) to read word by word. However, more seasoned readers should be capable of reading blocks of words. If you really think about how you read naturally, you'll likely discover that you already read a group of

several words at a time, with your eyes constantly scanning ahead of where you think you are in the text. Developing this natural tendency is key to successful speed-reading.

3. **Use your peripheral vision.** Typically, you might read a chunk of four or five words at a time. However, it shouldn't be difficult to increase this figure. Why not try holding this book further away from you than you might normally and relaxing your gaze. This is a simple way to absorb more words into your standard 'chunk'. Similarly, your peripheral vision might even take in the end of a line while you're still reading the middle of it.

4. **Focus on key words.** Although every word serves a purpose, some are more important than others. For example, if you focus on nouns and verbs, you'll likely get a better sense of a sentence than if you focus on conjunctions, prepositions and even adverbs and adjectives (don't panic – more on these in section two).

5. **Don't sub-vocalize.** This is the process by which we silently say each word in our head as we read it. Although it's a great trick for those first learning to read, the more proficient reader will benefit from breaking the habit because your brain understands a word quicker than you're able to say it. Indeed, there's strong evidence that many of us don't read every letter of each word as we scan a passage of text. Often we only need the first and last letters of each word in order to understand it. Read the following and see if you can work out what it says:

Ylo'ul psisolby mkae snese of tihs scentne eevn tughoh all the lteetrs are jmulbed.

While some people will see only gibberish, a great many will be able to read its meaning perfectly. (It should actually read: You'll possibly make sense of this sentence even though all the letters are jumbled.)

6. **Avoid 'regression'.** This means trying not to go back over text to check you read it correctly. Rather than consolidating your understanding, this tends to break the flow of concentration and decreases your overall comprehension. Only go back if you really need to.
7. **Use the tools provided.** Use any indicators within the text, such as headings or bullet points, for quick recognition.
8. **Use a finger to trace your reading.** It may feel child-like but it does help to keep your eye focussed on precisely where you are in the text, which helps to increase your pace.

On Your Marks: Putting Your Skills to the Test

Now it's time to test your speed-reading abilities. The questions in this section will check your factual recall to see how effectively you've absorbed the information. Each passage that follows has been given a designated reading time. Once you've finished the passage, don't attempt to answer the questions for at least five minutes.

Exercise 1

From *The Great Gatsby* by F. Scott Fitzgerald (1925)

Allow yourself thirty seconds to read this passage.

There was dancing now on the canvas in the garden, old men pushing young girls backward in eternal graceless circles, superior couples holding each other tortuously, fashionably and keeping in the corners – and a great number of single girls dancing individualistically or relieving the orchestra for a moment of the burden of the banjo or the traps. By midnight the hilarity had increased. A celebrated tenor had sung in Italian and a notorious contralto had sung in jazz and between the numbers people were doing 'stunts' all over the garden, while happy vacuous bursts of laughter rose toward the summer sky. A pair of stage 'twins' – who turned out to be the girls in yellow – did a baby act in costume and champagne was served in glasses bigger than finger bowls. The moon had risen higher, and floating in the Sound was a triangle of silver scales, trembling a little to the stiff, tinny drip of the banjos on the lawn.

I was still with Jordan Baker. We were sitting at a table with a man of about my age and a rowdy little girl who gave way upon the slightest provocation to uncontrollable laughter. I was enjoying myself now. I had taken two finger bowls of champagne and the scene had changed before my eyes into something significant, elemental and profound.

1) Two specific types of singer are described. Name them.
2) Which musical instruments are mentioned?
3) What colour outfits were the 'twins' wearing?
4) With whom was the narrator sat?

Exercise 2

From *The Woman in White* by Wilkie Collins (1860)

Allow yourself ninety seconds to read this passage.

It was the last day of July. The long hot summer was drawing to a close; and we, the weary pilgrims of the London pavement, were beginning to think of the cloud-shadows on the corn-fields, and the autumn breezes on the sea-shore.

For my own poor part, the fading summer left me out of health, out of spirits, and, if the truth must be told, out of money as well. During the past year I had not managed my professional resources as carefully as usual; and my extravagance now limited me to the prospect of spending the autumn economically between my mother's cottage at Hampstead and my own chambers in town.

The evening, I remember, was still and cloudy; the London air was at its heaviest; the distant hum of the street-traffic was at its faintest; the small pulse of the life within me, and the great heart of the city around me, seemed to be sinking in unison, languidly and more languidly, with the sinking sun. I roused myself from the book which I was dreaming over rather than reading, and left my chambers to meet the cool night air in the suburbs. It was one of the two evenings in every week which I was accustomed to spend with my mother and my sister. So I turned my steps northward in the direction of Hampstead.

Events which I have yet to relate make it necessary to mention in this place that my father had been dead some years at the period of which I am now writing; and that my sister Sarah and I were the sole survivors of a family of five children. My father was a drawing-master before me. His exertions had made him highly successful in his profession; and his affectionate anxiety to provide for the future of those who were dependent on his labours had impelled him, from the time of his marriage, to devote to the insuring of his life a much larger portion of his income than most men consider it necessary to set aside for that purpose. Thanks to his admirable prudence and self-denial my mother and sister were left, after his death, as independent of the world as they had been during his lifetime. I succeeded to his connection, and had every reason to feel grateful for the prospect that awaited me at my starting in life.

1) The fading summer rendered the speaker deficient in three things. What were they?
2) Where was the narrator's mother's cottage?
3) How many nights a week did the narrator spend with his mother and sister?
4) How many of the narrator's siblings had died?
5) What was the narrator's sister's name?

Exercise 3

From *Rapunzel* by The Brothers Grimm (1812, translation by Edgar Taylor and Marian Edwardes, 1912)

Allow yourself seventy-five seconds to read this passage.

There were once a man and a woman who had long in vain wished for a child. At length the woman hoped that God was about to grant her desire. These people had a little window at the back of their house from which a splendid garden could be seen, which was full of the most beautiful flowers and herbs. It was, however, surrounded by a high wall, and no one dared to go into it because it belonged to an enchantress, who had great power and was dreaded by all the world. One day the woman was standing by this window and looking down into the garden, when she saw a bed which was planted with the most beautiful rampion (rapunzel), and it looked so fresh and green that she longed for it, she quite pined away, and began to look pale and miserable. Then her husband was alarmed, and asked: 'What ails you, dear wife?' 'Ah,' she replied, 'if I can't eat some of the rampion, which is in the garden behind our house, I shall die.' The man, who loved her, thought: 'Sooner than let your wife die, bring her some of the rampion yourself, let it cost what it will.' At twilight, he clambered down over the wall into the garden of the enchantress, hastily clutched a handful of rampion, and took it to his wife. She at once made herself a salad of it, and ate it greedily. It tasted so good to her – so very good, that the next day she longed for it three times as much as before. If he was to have any rest, her husband must once more descend into the garden. In the gloom of evening therefore, he let himself down again; but when he had clambered down the wall he was terribly afraid, for he saw the enchantress standing before him. 'How can you dare,' said she with an angry look, 'descend into my garden and steal my rampion like a thief? You shall suffer for it!' 'Ah,' answered he, 'let mercy take the place of justice, I only made up my mind to do it out of necessity. My wife saw your rampion from the window, and felt such a longing for it that she would have died if she had not got some to eat.' Then the enchantress allowed her anger to be softened, and said to him: 'If the case be as you say, I will allow you to take away with you as much rampion as you will, only I make one condition, you must give me the child which your wife will bring into the world; it shall be well treated, and I will care for it like a mother.' The man in his terror consented to everything, and when the woman was brought to bed, the enchantress appeared at once, gave the child the name of Rapunzel, and took it away with her.

1) Where was the window from which the couple could see the garden?

2) What grew in the garden?

3) What did the wife make out of the rampion her husband gave her?

4) How much more rampion did the wife want the day after eating her first helping?

5) How much rampion did the enchantress allow the husband in exchange for his child?

Exercise 4

From 'The Tame Bird Was in a Cage' by Rabindranath Tagore (1915)

Allow yourself forty-five seconds to read this passage.

The tame bird was in a cage, the free bird was in the forest.

They met when the time came, it was a decree of fate.

The free bird cries, 'O my love, let us fly to the wood.'

The cage bird whispers, 'Come hither, let us both live in the cage.'

Says the free bird, 'Among bars, where is there room to spread one's wings?'

'Alas,' cries the caged bird, 'I should not know where to sit perched in the sky.'

The free bird cries, 'My darling, sing the songs of the woodlands.'

The cage bird sings, 'Sit by my side, I'll teach you the speech of the learned.'

The forest bird cries, 'No, ah no! songs can never be taught.'

The cage bird says, 'Alas for me, I know not the songs of the woodlands.'

There love is intense with longing, but they never can fly wing to wing.

Through the bars of the cage they look, and vain is their wish to know each other.

They flutter their wings in yearning, and sing, 'Come closer, my love!'

The free bird cries, 'It cannot be, I fear the closed doors of the cage.'

The cage bird whispers, 'Alas, my wings are powerless and dead.'

1) Where was the free bird?
2) What songs does the free bird want to sing?
3) What does the cage bird promise to teach the free bird?
4) Why can't the caged bird ever fly free?

Exercise 5

From *The Voyage of the Beagle* by Charles Darwin (1839)

Allow yourself two minutes to read this passage.

After having been twice driven back by heavy south-western gales, Her Majesty's ship *Beagle*, a ten-gun brig, under the command of Captain Fitz Roy, R.N., sailed from Devonport on the 27th of December, 1831. The object of the expedition was to complete the survey of Patagonia and Tierra del Fuego, commenced under Captain King in 1826 to 1830 – to survey the shores of Chile, Peru, and of some islands in the Pacific – and to carry a chain of chronometrical measurements round the World. On the 6th of January we reached Teneriffe, but were prevented landing, by fears of our bringing the cholera: the next morning we saw the sun rise behind the rugged outline of the Grand Canary island, and suddenly illuminate the Peak of Teneriffe, whilst the lower parts were veiled in fleecy clouds. This was the first of many delightful days never to be forgotten. On the 16th of January, 1832, we anchored at Porto Praya, in St. Jago, the chief island of the Cape de Verd archipelago.

The neighbourhood of Porto Praya, viewed from the sea, wears a desolate aspect. The volcanic fires of a past age, and the scorching heat of a tropical sun, have in most places rendered the soil unfit for vegetation. The country rises in successive steps of table-land, interspersed with some truncate conical hills, and the horizon is bounded by an irregular chain of more lofty mountains. The scene, as beheld through the hazy atmosphere of this climate, is one of great interest; if, indeed, a person, fresh from sea, and who has just walked, for the first time, in a grove of cocoa-nut trees, can be a judge of anything but his own happiness. The island would generally be considered as very uninteresting, but to anyone accustomed only to an English landscape, the novel aspect of an utterly sterile land possesses a grandeur which more vegetation might spoil. A single green leaf can scarcely be discovered over wide tracts of the lava plains; yet flocks of goats, together with a few cows, contrive to exist. It rains very seldom, but during a short portion of the year heavy torrents fall, and immediately afterwards a light vegetation springs out of every crevice. This soon withers; and upon such naturally formed hay the animals live. It had not now rained for an entire year. When the island was discovered, the immediate neighbourhood of Porto Praya was clothed with trees, the reckless destruction of which has caused here, as at St. Helena, and at some of the Canary islands, almost entire sterility. The broad, flat-bottomed valleys, many of which serve during a few days only in the season as water-courses, are clothed with thickets of leafless bushes. Few living creatures inhabit these valleys. The commonest bird is a kingfisher (Dacelo Iagoensis), which tamely sits on the branches of the castor-oil plant, and thence darts on grasshoppers and lizards. It is brightly coloured, but not so beautiful as the European species: in its flight, manners, and place of habitation, which is generally in the driest valley, there is also a wide difference.

1) How many guns did H.M.S. *Beagle* have?
2) On which date did it sail from Devonport?
3) Where did the vessel reach on 6th January?
4) Which animals are specifically mentioned as living around Porto Praya?

Exercise 6

From *The Scarlet Letter* by Nathaniel Hawthorne (1850)

Allow yourself sixty seconds to read this passage.

When the young woman – the mother of this child – stood fully revealed before the crowd, it seemed to be her first impulse to clasp the infant closely to her bosom; not so much by an impulse of motherly affection, as that she might thereby conceal a certain token, which was wrought or fastened into her dress. In a moment, however, wisely judging that one token of her shame would but poorly serve to hide another, she took the baby on her arm, and with a burning blush, and yet a haughty smile, and a glance that would not be abashed, looked around at her townspeople and neighbours. On the breast of her gown, in fine red cloth, surrounded with an elaborate embroidery and fantastic flourishes of gold thread, appeared the letter A. It was so artistically done, and with so much fertility and gorgeous luxuriance of fancy, that it had all the effect of a last and fitting decoration to the apparel which she wore, and which was of a splendour in accordance with the taste of the age, but greatly beyond what was allowed by the sumptuary regulations of the colony.

The young woman was tall, with a figure of perfect elegance on a large scale. She had dark and abundant hair, so glossy that it threw off the sunshine with a gleam; and a face which, besides being beautiful from regularity of feature and richness of complexion, had the impressiveness belonging to a marked brow and deep black eyes. She was ladylike, too, after the manner of the feminine gentility of those days; characterised by a certain state and dignity, rather than by the delicate, evanescent, and indescribable grace which is now recognised as its indication. And never had Hester Prynne appeared more ladylike, in the antique interpretation of the term, than as she issued from the prison. Those who had before known her, and had expected to behold her dimmed and obscured by a disastrous cloud, were astonished, and even startled, to perceive how her beauty shone out, and made a halo of the misfortune and ignominy in which she was enveloped.

1) How is her smile described as she surveyed the towns people?
2) How did Hester Prynne try to hide the embroidered letter A at the beginning of the extract?
3) Where on her clothing was the symbolic letter A?
4) What colour are Hester's eyes?

COMPRENDE?
COMPREHENSION

The following exercises are less concerned with factual recall than with comprehension – that is to say, your broader understanding of the material. Comprehension skills are honed not only by regular and broad reading but also by the reader's willingness to mine their own stores of experience, knowledge and empathy. In this way, the reader moves beyond merely comprehending facts in a piece of text towards a far more rewarding understanding. So, in short, you've got to use your brain a little bit more!

PUTTING IT INTO CONTEXT: FILL IN THE GAPS

Comprehension involves grasping the context of a passage, hearing its tone and identifying subtle nuances, applying a broader knowledge of the world, of particular places and periods, and of striving to understand not only what is happening in the text but why. In short, a reader with great comprehension skills not only processes the words present in a text but also fills in the gaps in between.

Take Your Time:
Putting it into Practice

Unlike the previous exercises, there are no recommended timings for reading the extracts that follow. You should feel free to use the speed-reading skills you've been practising, but don't be tempted to rush yourself.

Exercise 7

From *The Lion, the Fox and the Beasts*, one of Aesop's Fables (*c.* 620–560 BC, translation by Joseph Jacobs, 1894)

The lion once gave out that he was sick unto death and summoned the animals to come and hear his last Will and Testament. So the goat came to the lion's cave, and stopped there listening for a long time. Then a sheep went in, and before she came out a calf came up to receive the last wishes of the Lord of the Beasts. But soon the lion seemed to recover, and came to the mouth of his cave, and saw the fox, who had been waiting outside for some time.

'Why do you not come to pay your respects to me?' said the lion to the fox. 'I beg your Majesty's pardon,' said the fox, 'but I noticed the track of the animals that have already come to you; and while I see many hoof-marks going in, I see none coming out. 'Til the animals that have entered your cave come out again I prefer to remain in the open air.'

1)   List the three animals that went into the lion's cave.

2) Summarize in no more than twenty words the moral of this fable.

3) What do you think the fox represents?

Exercise 8

From *The Wind in the Willows* by Kenneth Grahame (1908)

'Hullo, Mole!' said the Water Rat.

'Hullo, Rat!' said the Mole.

'Would you like to come over?' enquired the Rat presently.

'Oh, it's all very well to TALK,' said the Mole, rather pettishly, he being new to a river and riverside life and its ways.

The Rat said nothing, but stooped and unfastened a rope and hauled on it; then lightly stepped into a little boat which the Mole had not observed. It was painted blue outside and white within, and was just the size for two animals; and the Mole's whole heart went out to it at once, even though he did not yet fully understand its uses.

The Rat sculled smartly across and made fast. Then he held up his forepaw as the Mole stepped gingerly down. 'Lean on that!' he said. 'Now then, step lively!' and the Mole to his surprise and rapture found himself actually seated in the stern of a real boat.

'This has been a wonderful day!' said he, as the Rat shoved off and took to the sculls again. 'Do you know, I've never been in a boat before in all my life.'

'What?' cried the Rat, open-mouthed: 'Never been in a—you never—well I—what have you been doing, then?'

'Is it so nice as all that?' asked the Mole shyly, though he was quite prepared to believe it as he leant back in his seat and surveyed the cushions, the oars, the rowlocks, and all the fascinating fittings, and felt the boat sway lightly under him.

'Nice? It's the ONLY thing,' said the Water Rat solemnly, as he leant forward for his stroke. 'Believe me, my young friend, there is NOTHING – absolutely nothing – half so much worth doing as simply messing about in boats. Simply messing,' he went on dreamily: 'messing – about – in – boats; messing—'

'Look ahead, Rat!' cried the Mole suddenly.

It was too late. The boat struck the bank full tilt. The dreamer, the joyous oarsman, lay on his back at the bottom of the boat, his heels in the air.

1) Had Mole lived by the River long?

2) What do the following words mean in the context of this extract?
   a) pettishly
   b) sculled
   c) stroke

3) Is Rat older or younger than Mole? Give a reason for your answer.

4) What effect does the narrator achieve by describing Rat as 'the dreamer, the joyous oarsman' in the final line?

Exercise 9

From *The Story of a Common Soldier of Army Life in the Civil War, 1861–1865* by Leander Stillwell (1920)

On June 16 our brigade left Bethel for Jackson, Tennessee, a town on the Mobile and Ohio railroad, and about thirty-five or forty miles, by the dirt road, northwest of Bethel. On this march, like the preceding one, I did not carry my knapsack. It was about this time that most of the boys adopted the 'blanket-roll' system. Our knapsacks were awkward, cumbersome things, with a combination of straps and buckles that chafed the shoulders and back, and greatly augmented heat and general discomfort. So we would fold in our blankets an extra shirt, with a few other light articles, roll the blanket tight, double it over and tie the two ends together, then throw the blanket over one shoulder, with the tied ends under the opposite arm – and the arrangement was complete. We had learned by this time the necessity of reducing our personal baggage to the lightest possible limit. We had left Camp Carrollton with great bulging knapsacks, stuffed with all sorts of plunder, much of which was utterly useless to soldiers in the field. But we soon got rid of all that. And my recollection is that after the Bethel march the great majority of the men would, in some way, when on a march, temporarily lay aside their knapsacks, and use the blanket roll. The exceptions to that method, in the main, were the soldiers of foreign birth, especially the Germans. They carried theirs to the last on all occasions, with everything in them the army regulations would permit, and usually something more.

1) To which city had the soldiers decamped?
2) Why did the soldiers not have their knapsacks with them?
3) What did they use in replacement of the knapsacks?
4) Which soldiers, if any, kept their plunder?
5) Give the meaning of the following words as they are used in the passage:
   a) chafed
   b) augmented
   c) bulging
   d) plunder

Exercise 10

'Sonnet 29' by William Shakespeare (*c*.1609)

When, in disgrace with fortune and men's eyes,
I all alone beweep my outcast state
And trouble deaf heaven with my bootless cries
And look upon myself and curse my fate,
Wishing me like to one more rich in hope,
Featured like him, like him with friends possess'd,
Desiring this man's art and that man's scope,
With what I most enjoy contented least;
Yet in these thoughts myself almost despising,
Haply I think on thee, and then my state,
Like to the lark at break of day arising
From sullen earth, sings hymns at heaven's gate;
For thy sweet love remember'd such wealth brings
That then I scorn to change my state with kings.

1) In lines 5-7, the speaker envies various things that others have. Which of the following does he not mention?
   a) artistic ability; b) popularity; c) power; d) money
2) To what does the speaker compare his improved mood on thinking of his love?
3) Summarize the changing mood of the narrator throughout the poem in no more than fifty words.

Exercise 11

From *Gulliver's Travels* by Jonathan Swift (1726)

He is taller by almost the breadth of my nail, than any of his court; which alone is enough to strike an awe into the beholders. His features are strong and masculine, with an Austrian lip and arched nose, his complexion olive, his countenance erect, his body and limbs well proportioned, all his motions graceful, and his deportment majestic. He was then past his prime, being twenty-eight years and three quarters old, of which he had reigned about seven in great felicity, and generally victorious. For the better convenience of beholding him, I lay on my side, so that my face was parallel to his, and he stood but three yards off: however, I have had him since many times in my hand, and therefore cannot be deceived in the description. His dress was very plain and simple, and the fashion of it between the Asiatic and the European; but he had on his head a light helmet of gold, adorned with jewels, and a plume on the crest. He held his sword drawn in his hand to defend himself, if I should happen to break loose; it was almost three inches long; the hilt and scabbard were gold enriched with diamonds. His voice was shrill, but very clear and articulate; and I could distinctly hear it when I stood up. The ladies and courtiers were all most magnificently clad; so that the spot they stood upon seemed to resemble a petticoat spread upon the ground, embroidered with figures of gold and silver. His imperial majesty spoke often to me, and I returned answers: but neither of us could understand a syllable. There were several of his priests and lawyers present (as I conjectured by their habits), who were commanded to address themselves to me; and I spoke to them in as many languages as I had the least smattering of, which were High and Low Dutch, Latin, French, Spanish, Italian, and Lingua Franca, but all to no purpose.

1) This passage describes Gulliver's impressions of the Emperor of Lilliput. What colour skin does the emperor have?
2) What is an Austrian lip?
3) How does the description of the Emperor's weaponry emphasize his diminutive stature?
4) Give alternatives to the following words used in the passage:
    a) deportment
    b) conjectured
    c) smattering

Exercise 12

'Because I could not stop for Death' by Emily Dickinson (first printed 1890)

Because I could not stop for Death,
He kindly stopped for me;
The carriage held but just ourselves
And Immortality.

We slowly drove, he knew no haste,
And I had put away
My labor and my leisure too,
For His civility.

We passed the school, where children strove
At recess, in the ring;
We passed the fields of gazing grain,
We passed the Setting Sun.

Or rather, he passed us;
The dews drew quivering and chill,
For only gossamer my gown,
My tippet only tulle.

We paused before a house that seemed
A swelling of the ground;
The roof was scarcely visible,
The cornice-in the ground.

Since then 'tis Centuries, and yet each

Feels shorter than the day
I first surmised the horses' heads
Were toward eternity.

1) Give definitions for the following words:
    a) civility
    b) strove
    c) quivering
2) Can you detect the change in tense towards the end of
    the poem?
3) Why do you think the tense has changed from past
    to present?

Exercise 13

From *Dr Jekyll and Mr Hyde* by Robert Louis Stevenson (1886)

A maid servant living alone in a house not far from the river, had
gone up-stairs to bed about eleven. Although a fog rolled over the
city in the small hours, the early part of the night was cloudless, and
the lane, which the maid's window overlooked, was brilliantly lit by
the full moon. It seems she was romantically given, for she sat down
upon her box, which stood immediately under the window, and
fell into a dream of musing. Never (she used to say, with streaming
tears, when she narrated that experience), never had she felt more
at peace with all men or thought more kindly of the world. And
as she so sat she became aware of an aged and beautiful gentleman
with white hair, drawing near along the lane; and advancing to meet

him, another and very small gentleman, to whom at first she paid less attention. When they had come within speech (which was just under the maid's eyes) the older man bowed and accosted the other with a very pretty manner of politeness. It did not seem as if the subject of his address were of great importance; indeed, from his pointing, it sometimes appeared as if he were only inquiring his way; but the moon shone on his face as he spoke, and the girl was pleased to watch it, it seemed to breathe such an innocent and old-world kindness of disposition, yet with something high too, as of a well-founded self-content. Presently her eye wandered to the other, and she was surprised to recognise in him a certain Mr. Hyde, who had once visited her master and for whom she had conceived a dislike. He had in his hand a heavy cane, with which he was trifling; but he answered never a word, and seemed to listen with an ill-contained impatience. And then all of a sudden he broke out in a great flame of anger, stamping with his foot, brandishing the cane, and carrying on (as the maid described it) like a madman.

1) At what time does the scene depicted take place?
2) Do you think the events described happened in the narrator's recent past or longer ago? Give a reason for your answer?
3) What is meant by the phrase 'come within speech'?
4) The author uses particular phrases that encourage us to be sympathetic to the man whom Mr Hyde met. Identify two such phrases?

Exercise 14

From *The Adventure of the Engineer's Thumb* by Arthur Conan Doyle (1892)

It was in the summer of '89, not long after my marriage, that the events occurred which I am now about to summarise. I had returned to civil practice and had finally abandoned Holmes in his Baker Street rooms, although I continually visited him and occasionally even persuaded him to forgo his Bohemian habits so far as to come and visit us. My practice had steadily increased, and as I happened to live at no very great distance from Paddington Station, I got a few patients from among the officials. One of these, whom I had cured of a painful and lingering disease, was never weary of advertising my virtues and of endeavouring to send me on every sufferer over whom he might have any influence.

One morning, at a little before seven o'clock, I was awakened by the maid tapping at the door to announce that two men had come from Paddington and were waiting in the consulting-room. I dressed hurriedly, for I knew by experience that railway cases were seldom trivial, and hastened downstairs. As I descended, my old ally, the guard, came out of the room and closed the door tightly behind him.

'I've got him here,' he whispered, jerking his thumb over his shoulder; 'he's all right.'

'What is it, then?' I asked, for his manner suggested that it was some strange creature which he had caged up in my room.

'It's a new patient,' he whispered. 'I thought I'd bring him round myself; then he couldn't slip away. There he is, all safe and sound. I must go now, Doctor; I have my dooties, just the same as you.' And off he went, this trusty tout, without even giving me time to thank him.

1) What is the chief setting of this passage?
2) Do you think the new patient came to see the narrator willingly?
3) What do you understand to be meant by the term Bohemian as used in this passage?

Exercise 15

'To Autumn' by John Keats (1820)

Season of mists and mellow fruitfulness,
Close bosom-friend of the maturing sun,
Conspiring with him how to load and bless
With fruit the vines that round the thatch-eves run;
To bend with apples the mossed cottage-trees,
And fill all fruit with ripeness to the core;
To swell the gourd, and plump the hazel shells
With a sweet kernel; to set budding more,
And still more, later flowers for the bees,
Until they think warm days will never cease,
For Summer has o'er-brimmed their clammy cells.

Who hath not seen thee oft amid thy store?

Sometimes whoever seeks abroad may find
Thee sitting careless on a granary floor,
Thy hair soft-lifted by the winnowing wind;
Or on a half-reaped furrow sound asleep,
Drowsed with the fume of poppies, while thy hook
Spares the next swath and all its twinèd flowers;
And sometimes like a gleaner thou dost keep
Steady thy laden head across a brook;
Or by a cider-press, with patient look,
Thou watchest the last oozings hours by hours.

Where are the songs of Spring? Ay, where are they?
Think not of them, thou hast thy music too—
While barrèd clouds bloom the soft-dying day,
And touch the stubble-plains with rosy hue:
Then in a wailful choir the small gnats mourn
Among the river sallows, borne aloft
Or sinking as the light wind lives or dies;
And full-grown lambs loud bleat from hilly bourn;
Hedge-crickets sing; and now with treble soft
The red-breast whistles from a garden-croft;
And gathering swallows twitter in the skies.

1)   Give definitions for the following words:
     a)   wailful
     b)   winnowing
     c)   clammy

2) In the second stanza, autumn is likened to a gleaner. What is a gleaner?

3) How do the last two lines suggest the imminent arrival of winter?

Exercise 16

From *The Diary of Samuel Pepys* (1825)

September, 1666

2nd (Lord's day). Some of our mayds sitting up late last night to get things ready against our feast today, Jane called us up about three in the morning, to tell us of a great fire they saw in the City. So I rose and slipped on my nightgowne, and went to her window, and thought it to be on the backside of Marke-lane at the farthest; but, being unused to such fires as followed, I thought it far enough off; and so went to bed again and to sleep. About seven rose again to dress myself, and there looked out at the window, and saw the fire not so much as it was and further off. So to my closet to set things to rights after yesterday's cleaning. By and by Jane comes and tells me that she hears that above 300 houses have been burned down tonight by the fire we saw, and that it is now burning down all Fish Street, by London Bridge. So I made myself ready presently, and walked to the Tower, and there got up upon one of the high places, Sir J. Robinson's little son going up with me; and there I did see the houses at that end of the bridge all on fire, and an infinite great fire on this and the other side the end of the bridge; which, among other people, did trouble me for poor little Michell and our

Sarah on the bridge. So down, with my heart full of trouble, to the Lieutenant of the Tower, who tells me that it begun this morning in the King's baker's house in Pudding-lane, and that it hath burned St. Magnus's Church and most part of Fish Street already.

1) At what time of day did Pepys get up and dressed?
2) Who was Jane and why was she awake?
3) In what sort of building did the fire begin?
4) Why did Pepys go back to bed after initially seeing the fire?

Exercise 17

From *Alice's Adventures in Wonderland* by Lewis Carroll (1865)

Alice was beginning to get very tired of sitting by her sister on the bank, and of having nothing to do: once or twice she had peeped into the book her sister was reading, but it had no pictures or conversations in it, 'and what is the use of a book,' thought Alice, 'without pictures or conversation?'

So she was considering in her own mind (as well as she could, for the hot day made her feel very sleepy and stupid), whether the pleasure of making a daisy-chain would be worth the trouble of getting up and picking the daisies, when suddenly a White Rabbit with pink eyes ran close by her.

There was nothing so VERY remarkable in that; nor did Alice think it so VERY much out of the way to hear the Rabbit say to itself, 'Oh dear! Oh dear! I shall be late!' (when she thought it over afterwards, it occurred to her that she ought to have wondered at this, but at the time it all seemed quite natural); but when the Rabbit actually TOOK A WATCH OUT OF ITS WAISTCOAT-POCKET, and looked at it, and then hurried on, Alice started to her feet, for it flashed across her mind that she had never before seen a rabbit with either a waistcoat-pocket, or a watch to take out of it, and burning with curiosity, she ran across the field after it, and fortunately was just in time to see it pop down a large rabbit-hole under the hedge.

In another moment down went Alice after it, never once considering how in the world she was to get out again.

1) Where is Alice at the beginning of this passage?
2) What evidence is there to suggest that Alice may be dreaming?
3) The White Rabbit is given human characteristics (e.g. he wears clothes, carries a watch and speaks). What term is used to describe the attribution of human characteristics to other animals?

Exercise 18

From *Moby Dick* by Herman Melville (1851)

At the period of our arrival at the Island, the heaviest storage of the *Pequod* had been almost completed; comprising her beef, bread, water, fuel, and iron hoops and staves. But, as before hinted, for some time there was a continual fetching and carrying on board of divers odds and ends of things, both large and small.

Chief among those who did this fetching and carrying was Captain Bildad's sister, a lean old lady of a most determined and indefatigable spirit, but withal very kindhearted, who seemed resolved that, if SHE could help it, nothing should be found wanting in the *Pequod*, after once fairly getting to sea. At one time she would come on board with a jar of pickles for the steward's pantry; another time with a bunch of quills for the chief mate's desk, where he kept his log; a third time with a roll of flannel for the small of someone's rheumatic back. Never did any woman better deserve her name, which was Charity – Aunt Charity, as everybody called her. And like a sister of charity did this charitable Aunt Charity bustle about hither and thither, ready to turn her hand and heart to anything that promised to yield safety, comfort, and consolation to all on board a ship in which her beloved brother Bildad was concerned, and in which she herself owned a score or two of well-saved dollars.

But it was startling to see this excellent hearted Quakeress coming on board, as she did the last day, with a long oil-ladle in one hand, and a still longer whaling lance in the other. Nor was

Bildad himself nor Captain Peleg at all backward. As for Bildad, he carried about with him a long list of the articles needed, and at every fresh arrival, down went his mark opposite that article upon the paper. Every once in a while Peleg came hobbling out of his whalebone den, roaring at the men down the hatchways, roaring up to the riggers at the mast-head, and then concluded by roaring back into his wigwam.

1) What do you think the *Pequod* might be?
2) What do you think the author means by the term 'backward'?
3) Explain in your own words what the author means by the word 'roaring'.

Exercise 19

From *The Adventures of Tom Sawyer* by Mark Twain (1876)

Within two minutes, or even less, he had forgotten all his troubles. Not because his troubles were one whit less heavy and bitter to him than a man's are to a man, but because a new and powerful interest bore them down and drove them out of his mind for the time – just as men's misfortunes are forgotten in the excitement of new enterprises. This new interest was a valued novelty in whistling, which he had just acquired from a negro, and he was suffering to practise it un-disturbed. It consisted in a peculiar bird-like turn, a sort of liquid warble, produced by touching the tongue to the roof of the mouth at short intervals in the midst of the music –

the reader probably remembers how to do it, if he has ever been a boy. Diligence and attention soon gave him the knack of it, and he strode down the street with his mouth full of harmony and his soul full of gratitude. He felt much as an astronomer feels who has discovered a new planet – no doubt, as far as strong, deep, unalloyed pleasure is concerned, the advantage was with the boy, not the astronomer.

The summer evenings were long. It was not dark, yet. Presently Tom checked his whistle. A stranger was before him – a boy a shade larger than himself. A new comer of any age or either sex was an impressive curiosity in the poor little shabby village of St. Petersburg. This boy was well dressed, too – well dressed on a week-day. This was simply astounding. His cap was a dainty thing, his close-buttoned blue cloth roundabout was new and natty, and so were his pantaloons. He had shoes on – and it was only Friday. He even wore a necktie, a bright bit of ribbon. He had a citified air about him that ate into Tom's vitals. The more Tom stared at the splendid marvel, the higher he turned up his nose at his finery and the shabbier and shabbier his own outfit seemed to him to grow. Neither boy spoke. If one moved, the other moved – but only sidewise, in a circle; they kept face-to-face and eye-to-eye all the time. Finally Tom said:

'I can lick you!'

'I'd like to see you try it.'

'Well, I can do it.'

'No you can't, either.'

1) Which of the following is the most appropriate alternative to the phrase 'one whit' that appears in the first paragraph:
   a) one ounce;
   b) on consideration;
   c) one iota?

2) What distracts Tom from his previous worries?

3) There are several clues that Tom's background is not a wealthy one. Give two examples.

4) What is meant by the word 'lick' in this context?

SECTION II
WRITING

Grammar: it's a word that sends a chill down the spine of the most hardy of fellows, but there's no need to worry. Broken down into manageable chunks, the art of writing proper English is, dare I say it, quite fun to learn. And, not only will this section give you the tools to be able to craft the perfect sentence, it'll also teach you how to present it beautifully, too.

ALL IN THE RIGHT ORDER
GRAMMAR

Now you're a speed-reading aficionado with masterful skills in comprehension, the time has come to test your written language skills. And the best place to begin is with every schoolboy's favourite: grammar.

PART AND PARCEL: PARTS OF SPEECH

Our alphabet contains twenty-six letters (five vowels – a, e, i, o and u – and twenty-one consonants), which can be arranged into hundreds of thousands of words. To give you some idea of how many hundreds of thousands there are, the Second Edition of the *Oxford English Dictionary* contains full entries for over 170,000 words currently in use.

Every word has its own meaning and purpose but each one can be classified, rather handily, into one of eight basic groups known as *parts of speech*.

Mix and Match

To get things started, I'd like to test your prior knowledge of the eight parts of speech. Match each part of speech listed in Column A with its correct definition from Column B and appropriate examples from Column C. Don't forget to write your answers on a separate sheet of paper.

Exercise 1

Column A	Column B	Column C
1) Noun	A word that adds meaning to a verb. _Adverb_	On, behind, during _preposition_
2) Verb	A 'naming' word for a person, thing or place. _Noun_	You, us, something _pronoun_
3) Pronoun	A 'doing' word that describes an action or a state of being. _Verb_	Yikes, hurrah, shh _Interjection_
4) Adjective	A 'stand-alone' word that expresses emotion. _Interjection_	Until, and, though _Conjunction_
5) Adverb	A word used before a noun or pronoun to express the _preposition_ relationship between it and another object.	Beautiful, colourful, broken _adjective_
6) Preposition	A word used as a substitute for a noun, usually referring to a participant in the sentence or a noun already mentioned. _Pronoun_	Car, dog, France _Noun_
7) Conjunction	A word that describes a noun. _adjective_	Vaguely, avidly, slowly _Adverb_

8) Interjection	A 'joining' word that links together sentences, phrases or clauses. _conjunction_	To be, to drive, to swim _verb_

Exercise 2

Hopefully the previous exercise has shaken up those old brain cells and reminded you of the basics. But, as ever, there's no rest for the wicked – now it's time to consolidate that knowledge. In this exercise, write on a separate sheet of paper any examples of the parts of speech indicated in brackets at the end of each sentence.

1) I enjoy watching football. (Noun) _Football_
2) Jack knew himself very well but didn't trust them. (Pronoun)
3) Either we win the lottery or I'll have to go back to work. (Conjunction)
4) The pupil had the neatest handwriting in the school. (Adjective)
5) The dog sprinted across the beach. (Verb)
6) 'Good grief!' said the woman as she inspected her new haircut. (Interjection)
7) She despises custard with her apple pie. (Pronoun)
8) The sprinter rapidly accelerated. (Adverb)
9) The train chugged through the tunnel. (Preposition)

10) A shimmering diamond sat in the centre of the ring. (Adjective)

11) The injured man screamed piercingly. (Adverb)

12) The nuns ran over the hill. (Preposition)

13) My family went to the theatre. (Noun)

14) He was talented but lacked application. (Conjunction)

15) The doctor concluded his examination. (Verb)

16) The prima ballerina returned to the stage amid calls of 'Encore! (Interjection)

Exercise 3

Bah! Humbug! More exercises, you say? I'm afraid so. Here's a short extract from the Charles Dickens classic *A Christmas Carol*. Can you identify which part of speech each of the underlined words is? Write your answers on a separate sheet of paper.

The door of Scrooge's counting-house was open that he might keep his eye upon his clerk, who in a dismal little cell beyond, a sort of tank, was copying letters. Scrooge had a very small fire, but the clerk's fire was so very much smaller that it looked like one coal. But he couldn't replenish it, for Scrooge kept the coal-box in his own room; and so surely as the clerk came in with the shovel, the master predicted that it would be necessary for them to part. Wherefore the clerk put on his white comforter, and tried to warm himself at the candle; in which effort, not being a man of a strong imagination, he failed.

'A merry Christmas, uncle! God save <u>you</u>!' <u>cried</u> a cheerful voice. It was the voice <u>of</u> Scrooge's nephew, who came upon him so quickly that this was the first intimation he had of his approach.

'<u>Bah!</u>' said Scrooge, 'Humbug!'

NAME THAT THING: NOUNS

As we've seen, nouns are used to name things and without them we wouldn't be able to differentiate one object, person or place from another.

What's Your Type?

To complicate matters further, there are two principal types of noun:

- *Common nouns*, which are used to name a person, animal, place, thing or abstract concept. Common nouns can be further subdivided into:
  - *Concrete nouns*, which describe things that can be recognized by at least one of the senses. Examples of concrete nouns might include a tree, a zebra, a bell and a piece of cheese.
  - *Abstract nouns*, which describe something beyond the physical realm. For example, courage and laziness are both abstract nouns.
  - *Proper nouns*, which are used to name a specific person, animal, place or thing. You can usually spot them because they'll generally begin with a capital letter. For example, Germany, the Taj Mahal and Justin Bieber are all proper nouns.

Exercise 4

Have a look at the six statements that follow and decide whether the underlined word in each sentence is a concrete, abstract or proper noun.

1) He was a <u>delight</u> to teach. *abst.*
2) Fred wants to work for the <u>United Nations</u>. *proper*
3) He swam across the <u>dock</u>. *concrete*
4) The nice lady donated a <u>cake</u>. *concrete*
5) She was terrified of <u>failing</u>. *abstract*
6) When are we going to visit the <u>Louvre</u>? *proper*

Compound Interest

Just when you thought you'd got to grips with nouns, it turns out there are even more of them! A *compound noun* is a noun made up of two (and occasionally more) words to make a new word with a meaning all of its own. They usually comprise two nouns or a noun and an adjective (thus compound noun is itself a compound noun). They can be rendered as a single run-on word, two or more separate words or a phrase separated by a hyphen.

Exercise 5

Pair up the words from Column A with those in Column B to form ten compound nouns. Use each word only once.

	Column A	Column B
1)	Rattle	pool
2)	Country	on

3)	Green	side
4)	Pan	in
5)	Short	moon
6)	Hanger	house
7)	Swimming	cake
8)	Check	hand
9)	Over	snake
10)	Full	ripe

Count on It

All nouns can be described either as *countable* or *non-countable* (or *mass*) nouns. The rules governing these designations are pleasingly simple: if you can count them (e.g. chairs or tigers), they're countable, and if you can't (as with, say, milk or history), they're not. To be sure of the type of noun, just ask yourself 'how many?'

Exercise 6

Have a look at the following five nouns and decide if they're countable or non-countable.

1) Grief
2) Car
3) Sugar
4) Log
5) Garage

Much Ado

Quantifiers are words and phrases that indicate the volume or amount of something. The most familiar quantifiers are, of course, numbers. But often we need to talk in more general terms, as we've already seen in the case of non-countable nouns. For non-countable nouns we can use phrases such as *some*, *lots*, *a bit* and *not much*, while countable nouns have a few quantifiers of their own other than numbers (e.g. *many*, *a few*). Still other quantifiers work with both countables and non-countables. This group includes *enough* and *a lot of*. You should also note that the adjective *less* is used only with non-countables, while *fewer* works with countables.

Exercise 7

Complete the sentences that follow with the most appropriate quantifier from the list, using each only once. Don't forget to note down your answers on a separate sheet of paper.

> *a lot of   too few   too many   a few   a couple of*
> *a lack of   a little   less   too much*

1) He rushed his work and would have benefited from _____ haste.
2) She had _____ tickets for the gigs so asked her best friend along.
3) _____ people take exercise.
4) Though _____ the tapestry was destroyed,

_____ remained in perfect condition.

5)   _____ chocolate is bad for you.

6)   The friends went for _____ drinks.

7)   _____ rugby players get injured.

8)   For a diplomat, he had _____ tact.

Some Dos and Don'ts

Some and *any* are useful quantifiers governed by a few straightforward rules. Use *some* in:

* Positive sentences
  * e.g. We have some money.

* Offers
  * e.g. Do you need some money?

* Questions anticipating a positive response
  * e.g. Could I have some money?

Use *any* in:

* Negative sentences
  * e.g. We don't have any money.

* Questions other than those described above.
  * e.g. Is there any money in the safe?

Exercise 8

To make life a little simpler (for once) those other words based on the any- and some- stems (anybody/somebody, anyone/someone, anything/something, anywhere/somewhere) follow the same rules. So, on your separate sheet of paper, complete the following sentences with the most appropriate word from those in brackets.

1) Do you have _____ playing cards at home?
   (some/any)

3) Would _____ like to help me out?
   (somebody/anybody)

4) She didn't know _____ at her new school.
   (somebody/anybody)

5) Do you know _____ who can give us a lift?
   (someone/anyone)

6) You know _____ about this, don't you?
   (something/anything)

7) I couldn't sleep after I had _____ coffee.
   (some/any)

8) Is there _____ coffee in the pot?
   (some/any)

When One is Not Enough

To turn many words from the singular to the plural form, the simple addition of an -s at the end of the word suffices. In this way, for example, we talk about one car but two cars and one tree but two trees. However, in a great many cases, you'll need to work a bit harder:

- Add -es if a word already ends with:
  - an -s
  - an -x or -z sound
  - a -ch or -sh
  - with a -y preceded by a consonant (and turn the -y into an -i).

- Add -es for some words that end with an -o (e.g. avocado). However, this is not always the case (e.g. disco). You will simply have to learn which -o words are of which type as you go along.

- Add -ves if a word ends with -f (though not -ff) or -fe (e.g. thief or life). However, once again there are exceptions where a simple additional -s does the job (as with belief). A few words, such as roof, can be pluralized either way.

Exercise 9

Turn each of the following singulars into plurals. Be warned, some words follow the above rules more closely than others!

1)   French fry
2)   Day
3)   Tax
4)   Potato
5)   Hoof
6)   Quiz
7)   Fish
8)   Wife

Most Irregular!

There are a good many nouns in the English language – many of them derived from Latin, Greek and Old English – that don't add an -s at all. As if pluralizing needed further complication!

Exercise 10

Here are some singular nouns that pose special challenges when converting into the plural. How many can you correctly pluralize?

1)   Child
2)   Mouse
3)   Sheep
4)   Tooth

5) Ox
6) Stadium
7) Stimulus
8) Crisis
9) Woman
10) Index
11) Medium
12) Species

Group Thinking

A *collective noun* is used to describe a group of things or animals. Library, audience, class, fleet, jury and family are all examples of collective nouns. Many are part of everyday language, such as herd, the collective noun for cattle, flock for sheep and bouquet for flowers. Others, however, are used only rarely. Did you know, for example, that we have a parliament of owls and an unkindness of ravens?

Since the collective noun treats a collection of individuals as a single entity, it should normally take the singular verb (e.g. 'My class is going on a trip' not 'My class are going on a trip'). However, sometimes we refer to the actions of individuals within the group, in which case the noun takes the plural (e.g. 'The class were working on several different projects.'). Referring to the visit, the class is being treated as a unit; referring to the projects, the class is being treated as a collection of individuals.

Exercise 11

Use the appropriate form of the verb in each of the following sentences.

1) Most of the crew _____ killed in the crash. (was/were)

2) The crew _____ the most respected in the company. (was/were)

3) The audience _____ singing along with the chorus. (is/are)

4) Some of the audience _____ demanding refunds. (is/are)

5) The interview panel _____ interrogating the candidate. (was/were)

6) The interview panel _____ not in agreement about whom to appoint. (was/were)

Articulating Articles

An *article* is a short word that indicates what sort of reference is being made to the noun that comes after it. There are two types:

- *A* or *an* are the *indefinite articles* and indicate that the subject noun is being spoken about in general terms.

- *The* is the *definite article* and indicates that the subject is being spoken of in specific terms.

Study the following two statements:

- A man walked into my shop.

- The man walked into my shop.

In sentence one, the indefinite article shows that this was a random man, but the definite article in sentence two shows we're talking about a particular man. They may be short but articles express a lot of information.

Remember, the rule is to use *a* for the indefinite article in front of a word that begins with a consonant, but *an* if it starts with a vowel. However, as ever, there are one or two exceptions ...

- If a word begins with an *h* that is sounded, as in 'house', then use *a*. If the *h* is silent, as in 'hour', use *an*.

- If a word starts with a vowel that's sounded like a consonant, use *an*. For example, we would refer to 'a European' because 'European' begins with a 'Y'-sound.

- But if a word starts with a consonant that is sounded like a vowel use *an*, e.g. we refer to 'an MP' because the 'M' is sounded like a vowel (*Em*).

Often, place names don't require an article. We go to Paris, for example, not *the* Paris. Similarly, we might climb Mount Everest but not *the* Mount Everest. But sometimes *the* is required. Use it:

- For places with Republic, States or Kingdom as part of their name (e.g. the Czech Republic, the United States)

- For 'plural' names (e.g. the Philippines)

- With High Street (but not most other road names)

- For oceans, seas, rivers and canals

- For hotels, museums, theatres and cinemas

- For places containing an 'of' (e.g. the Tower of London)

- When describing a place in terms of the north/east/south/ west of somewhere else

Exercise 12

In the following pairs of sentences, decide which one better takes the definite article and which one the indefinite.

1) She is going to buy ___ hat for the wedding.
2) He looks ridiculous in ___ hat his wife bought him.
3) The Taj Mahal is ___ beautiful building.
4) The Taj Mahal is ___ best-known site in India.
5) Do you have ___ idea of the price?
6) Do you know the price of ___ loaf of bread?

Getting Personal

Pronouns can be used instead of having to repeat a noun several times close together. There are three main types of pronoun:

- Nominative – replacing a subject noun.

- Accusative – replacing an object noun.

- Possessive – replacing a possessive adjective (such as my or your) as well as the following noun or noun phrase (e.g. my book).

Below is a table of the basic *personal pronouns* for each of the three main cases:

Nominative	Accusative	Possessive
1st person singular	I, me	mine
2nd person singular	you, you	yours
3rd person singular	he, she, it	him, her, it
		his, hers,
		theirs
1st person plural	we, us	ours
2nd person plural	you	your
3rd person plural	they, them	theirs

Reflexive pronouns, meanwhile, are used in cases where the subject and object of a sentence are the same (e.g. Tom tripped *himself* up). They can also effectively add emphasis (e.g. I can't abide it, *myself*). To form reflexive pronouns, add -self to the singular personal pronouns and -selves to the plural forms.

Also useful are the two *reciprocal pronouns*, *each other* and *one another*. Each other indicates a reciprocal relationship between two people or things (e.g. The couple loved *each other*), while one another is used for numbers greater than two (e.g. The family loved *one another*).

Exercise 13

Rewrite the following rather clumsy sentences, replacing the words and phrases in bold with suitable pronouns.

1) Anna could not believe **Anna's** luck.
2) After scoring the winning goal, the team ran to the corner and celebrated with **the team**.
3) Did you do that to **you**?
4) Fred and Joe were best friends and spent all their time playing with **Fred and Joe**.
5) We bought **us** a new car.
6) If I had found the treasure it would be **my treasure** but they found **the treasure** so it's **their treasure**.

Theory of Relativity

The *relative pronouns* are *that*, *which*, *who*, *whom* and *whose*. We use them at the start of subordinate clauses – which, by definition, are separate to the sentence's main clause – that furnish extra information about the noun that immediately precedes the relative pronoun (or, in the case of *which*, the whole of the preceding clause). Although *which* and *that* are often used interchangeably, the general rule suggests that *which* should follow a comma and relates to a whole clause, while *that* covers the noun only and does not require a comma.

When to use *who*, *who's*, *whose* and *whom* is a source of great confusion for many English speakers. So what are the rules?

- *Who* is the subjective relative pronoun.

- *Whom* is the objective relative pronoun.

- *Whose* is the possessive relative pronoun.

- *Who's* is not strictly a pronoun at all, but a contraction of *who is*.

Exercise 14

Fill in the gaps in the following sentences with an appropriate relative pronoun, using each only once. Beware, one sentence takes *who's*.

> *that   which   who   whom   who's   whose*

1) The breaded chicken, _____ was filled with garlic butter, was over-cooked.

2) He _____ lives in a glass house should not throw stones.

3) I was invited to a party for my neighbour _____ about to turn ninety.

4) The judges gave a prize to the person _____ marrow was largest.

5) The beach _____ we visited was beautiful.

6) _____ did he decide to invite to the show?

Asking the Question

The words *what, which, who, whose* and *whom* (sometimes used with the suffixes *-ever* and *-soever* as well) can be used in place of nouns to form certain sorts of questions. In this context, these words are known as *interrogative pronouns*. As with relative pronouns, *whom* is used in reference to the object rather than the subject of a sentence, and *whose* is the possessive form of *who*.

Exercise 15

Read the following statements and then re-write the questions using the most appropriate interrogative pronoun.

1)   This is the Queen's palace.

    _____ palace is this?

2)   I am addressing this letter to him.

    To _____ should I address this letter?

3)   Charles Dickens wrote *Oliver Twist*.

    _____ wrote *Oliver Twist*?

4)   I am carrying a brief case.

    _____ are you carrying?

5)   I think Usain Bolt will win the race.

    _____ sprinter do you think will win the race?

Generally Speaking

When you don't want to or are unable to refer to a specific noun, you can use an *indefinite pronoun* instead. Common examples include *all*, *any*, *anything*, *everyone*, *a few*, *no one*, *one*, *several*, *someone* and *something*.

Demonstrative pronouns, meanwhile, can be used to indicate something without actually naming it. We use *this* and *that* for singular nouns and *these* and *those* for plurals. *This* and *that* also signify nearness (both in terms of time and space) while *these* and *those* imply something further away.

Exercise 16

Look at the following sentences and fill in each gap with the most suitable example of the pronoun types indicated in brackets.

1) _____ can turn back the clock. (indefinite pronoun)
2) I must buy her _____ for her birthday. (indefinite pronoun)
3) I want _____ one over there. (demonstrative pronoun)
4) Are _____ on the table here all for me? (demonstrative pronoun)
5) Do you know _____ who can fix my car who won't charge too much? (indefinite pronoun)
6) I only meant to eat one cake but ended up having _____. (indefinite pronoun)
7) I can't choose just one because I love them _____.

(indefinite pronoun)

8) Were _____ your friends at the party last night?
    (demonstrative pronoun)

ALL ACTION: VERBS

Right, well done on getting this far. Now it's time to get to the heart of the action – while nouns tell us the subjects of a sentence, verbs tell us exactly what it is that's going on.

Regulate

Most verbs are *regular* and conform to a set of standard rules. This means that it's a fairly simple job to conjugate them (i.e. change their form to indicate person, tense, mood and number). In fact, if you know a verb's *infinitive* form (the most basic form of a verb, consisting of the verb preceded by *to*) plus the *past* and *present participle* forms, you're all set to undertake all the conjugation you wish. *Conjugate* is itself a regular verb and here are its three key forms:

Infinitive	**Past participle**	**Present participle**
to conjugate	conjugated	conjugating

(NB Because *conjugate* ends with an -*e*, it requires only the addition of a -*d* in the past participle form but the -*e* drops off to be replaced by -*ing* in the present participle. A verb not ending in an -*e*, such as *call*, simply takes an -*ed* in the past participle and an -*ing* in the present participle).

70

Alas, English is a funny old language, full of verbs that are *irregular*, which makes the process of conjugating a little more tricky. These *irregular verbs* include some of the most important, such as *to be*, *to have*, *to do* and *to go*. Sorry to be the bearer of bad news, but when it comes to regulating these verbs there are no short cuts to be made – they simply need to be learned.

Exercise 17

For each of these four key verbs, attempt to complete the table below. As usual, write your answers on a separate sheet of paper.

	To be	To have	To do	To go
	Present	Present	Present	Present
I	_____	_____	_____	_____
You	_____	_____	_____	_____
He/she/it	_____	_____	_____	_____
We	_____	_____	_____	_____
You	_____	_____	_____	_____
They	_____	_____	_____	_____
	Past	Past	Past	Past
I	_____	_____	_____	_____
You	_____	_____	_____	_____
He/she/it	_____	_____	_____	_____
We	_____	_____	_____	_____
You	_____	_____	_____	_____
They	_____	_____	_____	_____

Present participle   _____ _____ _____ _____
Past participle   _____ _____ _____ _____

Exercise 18

Those may be the most important of the irregular verbs but there are plenty more to keep them company. Some others are listed below. Can you work out how to form the *simple past* – simple because it has no need for an auxiliary verb (more on these on page 82), e.g. I won, you took – and the *past participle* in each case?

Infinitive	Past simple	Past participle
To arise	_____	_____
To bear	_____	_____
To become	_____	_____
To blow	_____	_____
To burst	_____	_____
To buy	_____	_____
To catch	_____	_____
To choose	_____	_____
To cut	_____	_____
To do	_____	_____
To draw	_____	_____
To drive	_____	_____
To eat	_____	_____
To fall	_____	_____
To fly	_____	_____
To forget	_____	_____
To give	_____	_____

To grow	_____	_____
To hide	_____	_____
To keep	_____	_____
To lie	_____	_____
To mistake	_____	_____
To read	_____	_____
To ring	_____	_____
To see	_____	_____
To shake	_____	_____
To speak	_____	_____
To swell	_____	_____
To take	_____	_____
To tear	_____	_____
To throw	_____	_____
To write	_____	_____

Building Blocks

So what should we do with all these nouns and verbs? Well, now we can set about forming the most basic sentences. The shortest sentence in the King James Bible, as an example, consists of only two words: 'Jesus wept.' Grammatically speaking, *Jesus* is the subject noun of the sentence and *wept* the verb. The next most basic sentence structure adds an object noun too. Take a look at the following sentence:

'He flies aeroplanes.'

Here, *he* is the subject (the one doing the verb), *flies* the verb, and *aeroplanes* the object (the one affected by the action).

Exercise 19

On a separate sheet of paper mark the subject and object in each case in the sentences below.

1) Shakespeare wrote plays.
2) I like to write my correspondence on a typewriter.
3) The window cleaner began his round at six in the morning.
4) The window cleaner's wife prepared his accounts for him.
5) The driver crashed his bus into a bus stop.

A subject noun and its verb should always be in agreement. That is to say, if the noun is in the singular then the verb should be likewise, while a plural noun goes with the plural form of the verb. Hence:

- *I am* happy.

- *We are* happy.

However, there are, as ever, several complications to take into account:

- If two nouns are joined by the conjunction *and*, the verb should go in the plural.
  - My friend *and* he *are* writing a play together.

- A conjugation implying the subjects are not doing the same thing accompanies a verb in the singular.
  - Do you know if Jack Spratt *or* his wife *is* going to eat fat?

- *Either/or* and *neither/nor* constructions demand the singular.

- *Anybody, anyone, everybody, everyone, somebody, someone, each, every* and *one* take the singular.

- *A few, both,* and *several* take the plural.

- *All, any, most* and *some* take the singular if used in conjunction with non-countable nouns but take the plural with countable nouns. Are you still with me? Good.

- Numerical expressions (such as collective nouns) can take either the singular or the plural, depending on whether the noun is being thought of as a single unit or as a collection of individuals.

- An intervening subordinate clause does not affect the verb.
    - My wife, as well as her sister, *is* a keen fan of Abba.

Exercise 20

In this exercise, let's add an *indirect object* to proceedings. An indirect object is the recipient of a direct object. So in the sentence 'He paid her a compliment', the *compliment* is the direct object and *her* is the indirect object. In the four sentences that follow, simply identify the indirect object.

1) The postman delivered her a letter.
2) The monarch awarded the soldier a bravery medal.
3) Tom ordered his team a new set of football strips.

4)   The lecturer showed his audience some slides.

Just as subject and verb should agree in terms of number, so subjects, objects and verbs should agree with each other in terms of case too. This does not usually present much of an issue until we're dealing with pronouns, so remember:

- Is there a 'missing' verb or are there other 'missing' words? If so, in some cases the pronoun should be in the nominative case, even though this sometimes feels counterintuitive. For example, we should say *He is wiser than I* rather than *He is wiser than me*. This is because what we're really saying is *He is wiser than I am*.

- However, some hidden verbs do take an object. For example, we would say *I admire her almost as much as him* because what we're really saying is *I admire her almost as much as I admire him*.

- If the personal pronoun follows *but*, it should be in the case it would have been in if the hidden verb were not hidden. So, while we might say *I waited five hours in the rain for tickets to Wimbledon. Who but I?* What we really mean is *Who but I would wait?*

Do As You Would Be Done To

Verbs can be subdivided into two categories:

- Transitive

- Intransitive

A *transitive verb* has at least one object while an *intransitive verb* has none. Consider these two statements:

- The boy laughed.

- The boy hit the ball.

In the first sentence, there is no object after the verb so *laugh* is intransitive. In the second sentence the ball is the object of the hitting, thus *hit* is transitive. Simple enough so far, except that some verbs are both transitive and intransitive. Take the verb *to eat*:

- All animals must eat.

- The old lady ate a slice of cake.

Both are perfectly good sentences but in the first line there is no need for a subject so the verb is intransitive, while in the second sentence, the slice of cake is the object, thus the verb is transitive.

Transitive verbs can be expressed in either the *active* or the *passive* voice. Simply put, the subject *does* in an active sentence, but the subject *is done* to in a passive one. Here are some music-related examples to elucidate:

- The boy strummed the guitar. (*Active*)

- The guitar was strummed. (*Short passive*)

- The guitar was strummed by the boy. (*Long passive*)

Exercise 21

The first three of the six sentences that follow are active and should be re-written as passive. The last three sentences are passive and should be re-written as active.

1) The grey horse ran the race.
2) The banker owns that Porsche.
3) The old lady visited the dentist.
4) The palace is inhabited by the king and his family.
5) The film star was chased down the street by the crowd.
6) *Far From the Madding Crowd* was written by Thomas Hardy.

All in Good Time

The tense of a verb informs us when the action being described happened or is happening. This will either be in the past, in the present or in the future. But bad luck if you think there are only three tenses to deal with. In fact, we use twelve in everyday English. They provide greater detail as to not only when exactly the action is occurring but also whether the action is over and done with speedily or else is ongoing. Let's take a look at each of the tenses in turn, using the regular verb *to learn*:

I learned	Simple past
I used to learn	Imperfect
I had learned	Past perfect
I was learning	Past continuous
I have learned	Present perfect
I learn	Present simple
I am learning	Present continuous
I have been learning	Present perfect continuous
I shall/will learn	Future simple
I shall/will have learned	Future perfect
I shall/will be learning	Future continuous
I shall/will have been learning	Future perfect continuous

Exercise 22

In the sentences that follow, replace the blank with the verb and tense indicated in the brackets at the end.

1) The policeman _____ a thief. (chase; present continuous)

2) We _____ to the nearest hospital. (drive; simple past)

3) I _____ dinner by the time you get home. (make; future perfect)

4) They _____ on the banks of the Ganges. (fish; past continuous)

5) He _____ fish and chips every Friday. (eat; present simple)

6) The tower _____ for four centuries next month. (stand; future perfect continuous)

7) They _____ the Greek myths. (study; present perfect continuous)

8) You _____ your Grandma every weekend. (visit; imperfect)

9) He _____ all his money at the casino. (lose; past perfect)

10) I _____ you a car if you pass your exams. (buy; future simple)

11) He _____ all his money in gold. (invest; present perfect)

12) They _____ the company by this time next year. (run; future continuous)

Where There's a Will

You'll often see *shall* and *will* used apparently indiscriminately in the formation of the future tense. However, there are several rules that subtly guard their usage, even if the modern world has all but forgotten them:

- Traditionally, *shall* is used for the first person and *will* for the second and third persons.

- When used with the first person singular or plural, *shall* expresses a simple statement of fact:
  - I shall go to the doctor's on Wednesday.

- Used with the second or third person singular or plural, *shall* implies a command, promise or strong assertion:
  - You shall hear from my solicitor.

- In questions, they affect the tone:
  - Shall I drive? (i.e. Would you like me to drive?)
  - Will I drive? (i.e. Am I going to drive?)

Exercise 23

Have a look at the following questions and decide whether each gap should be filled with *shall* or *will*.

1) 'You _____ follow the rules,' warned the referee sternly.
2) Rio _____ host the Olympics in 2016.
3) They announced they _____ be moving offices.

4) They _____ pay for this!

5) _____ we ever get out of this traffic jam?

6) _____ I get you a gift for your birthday?

Short and Sweet

Auxiliary verbs help to establish the tense, mood or voice of other verbs. The three main ones are *am*, *have* and *do*. Each of these, of course, works as a verb in its own right (e.g. I *have* a dog). But also supports other verbs (e.g. I *have walked* the dog). However, the other auxiliary verbs (*can, could, may, might, must, ought [to], shall, should, will, would*) need a main verb to have meaning.

Exercise 24

Mark the auxiliary verb in each of the following sentences.

1) I ought to go to the opticians.

2) The Queen has visited most of the world's countries.

3) He would kill to get tickets for the final.

4) You couldn't have made it up.

5) They do sing beautifully.

6) She can't say we didn't try.

In the Mood

When we talk about verbs having moods, what is it that we mean? It's not as if a word can be temperamental, after all. The mood of a verb is a tool we use to understand its context. There are three to bear in mind:

- *Indicative* – expressing a statement of fact or asking a question (e.g. I *like* chocolate. Do you *like* chocolate?).

- *Imperative* – expressing a command (e.g. *Get* me chocolate now!).

- *Subjunctive* – indicating an unreality or a hypothetical state, as when an action hasn't happened or doesn't exist (e.g. If you *were* made of chocolate...).

The subjunctive in particular has the power to confuse students of language. So let's take the opportunity to look at it in a little more detail. Don't be afraid, the subjunctive is your friend, not your foe – it's useful when we wish to talk about suppositions, hopes, desires, imaginings, doubts and suggestions. But how is it formed?

- The present subjunctive form differs from the regular present indicative in the third person singular only, where the *-s* is omitted at the end of the word. For example:
  - He goes running daily. (indicative)
  - She suggested that he *go* running with her. (subjunctive)

- The past subjunctive is exactly the same as the regular past indicative.

- With the verb *to be*, use *be* for all persons for the present subjunctive and *were* for the past subjunctive. For example:
  - I demand you *be* in attendance next week.
  - She wished she *were* a dress-size smaller.

- For all verbs, the future subjunctive is formed by *were* + the infinitive for all persons.
  - If *I were to do* the exam tomorrow, I would fail.

Exercise 25

Got that? Good. Now read the following sentences and determine the mood.

1) Have you ever been to Australia?
2) Don't walk on the grass!
3) I wouldn't eat that if I were you.
4) Take me to your leader.
5) If she were a bird, she'd be a nightingale.

Favourable Conditions

Just as subjunctives deal with 'things that aren't', so *conditionals* are sentence structures used with possible or imaginary – but not actual – situations. If you can grasp that, you're well on the way to mastering conditionals. By the way, that sentence beginning with 'If you can grasp that…' is an example of a conditional. There are two fundamental conditional forms:

- If something happens, something else happens.

- Something happens, if something else happens.

However, there are four types of conditional:

- *The zero conditional*, which describes a certainty at any time.
  - If you burn wood, it gets hot.

- *The first conditional*, which describes a likely proposition looking into the future.
  - If I sell my car, I will have to walk to work.

- *The second conditional*, which describes either an unlikely proposition looking into the future or an impossible proposition in the present.
  - If I discovered the secrets of alchemy, I would gold-plate my house.
  - If I had wings, I would fly to the moon.

- *The third conditional*, which describes something happening in the past different to what actually happened.
  - If I had revised more, I would have got a higher mark.

Exercise 26

Mark which conditional each of the following sentences is:

1) If I had known the truth, I would never have got involved.
2) If you jump out of an aeroplane, you will fall.
3) If I had nothing else to do, I would be a chess grand master.
4) If she buys a computer, she will get her work done more quickly.
5) If I found a million pounds, I would buy you a new house.

In the No

To turn a positive statement into a negative one when there's an auxiliary verb in play couldn't be simpler – we just have to add *not* after the auxiliary verb. So, for example, *I am cooking* becomes *I am not cooking* and *I have cooked* becomes *I have not cooked.*

However, if there's no auxiliary verb, default to *do* (in the appropriate tense) + *not* + the infinitive minus *to*. So, *I cook* becomes *I do not cook* and *I cooked* becomes *I did not cook.* There are a few other rules to remember:

- If *be* is the main verb, *not* follows *be*. So:
  - I am 21.
  - I *am not* 21.

- If *have* is the main verb, *do not* precedes have, e.g.:
  - He has a pink Cadillac.
  - He *does not have* a pink Cadillac.

- *Not* comes before infinitives and present participles. For example:
  - It is risky *not to be insured.*
  - The two dogs stared at each other, *not moving.*

It's a cardinal sin to over-use your negatives, since two negatives negate each other and create a positive. 'We're not even not bothered about that,' might the guilty double-negativers declare, little knowing that by not being not bothered, they are actually bothered! So don't ever do it. Not ever. Not 'not never'…

Exercise 27

Re-write the underlined words and phrases in the first six sentences that follow to make the sentences negative. The last three sentences contain examples of double negatives. Re-write those so that the double negative is removed but the intended meaning kept.

1) The weather <u>is good</u> today.
2) I <u>would like</u> to teach the world to sing.
3) I <u>always pay</u> my taxes on time.
4) My neighbours <u>keep</u> themselves to themselves.
5) The student turned over the exam paper, <u>panicking</u>.
6) It is tempting <u>to go</u>.
7) I don't know nothing.
8) There's not no one who deserves this more than you.
9) I wasn't nowhere near the crime scene.

Keeping It Brief

Sometimes it's neater and less formal to contract some of our *not* expressions. *Cannot*, for example, might be rendered as *can't* or *couldn't*, *do not* as *doesn't*, *don't* or *didn't*, *have not* as *hasn't*, *haven't* or *hadn't* and *be not* as *isn't*, *aren't* and *wasn't*. Most other auxiliary verbs can also take *n't*, with the exceptions of *shall* and *will* (which become *shan't* and *won't*, respectively). However, if you use a contraction in a question, you'll need to slightly adjust the word order. When using the uncontracted negative, the word order is: auxiliary verb + subject + not (e.g. Could you not see the sign?). When using the contracted form, the word order is: auxiliary verb + n't + subject (e.g. Couldn't you see the sign?).

Exercise 28

On a separate sheet of paper, re-write the following statements as negative questions, using the long and contracted forms. The first one is completed as an example.

1) We should visit.
    a)   Should we not visit?
    b)   Shouldn't we visit?

2) You could try asking.

3) You have eaten enough.

4) You are the prettiest of them all.

5) Shall we go out tonight.

−Ing the Swing

When using auxiliary verbs, we partner them with the *participle* form of the main verb. A participle on its own lacks information about person, tense, voice, mood and number. But in conjunction with an auxiliary, they help provide us with the full range of information.

The present participle, which is used for all continuous tenses, is easy to spot by the *-ing* ending it almost always has. To form the present participle, take the present continuous tense of a verb and take off the auxiliary form of *to be*. Thus, the present participle of *walk* is *walking* (present continuous: I am walking). In addition, the present participle can act as an adjective. For example, we might talk about *walking pace* or *walking stick*.

The past participle, meanwhile, usually (though not always) has one of the following endings: *-ed*, *-d*, *-t*, *-en* and *-n*. To form it, take the past perfect tense and knock off the auxiliary form of *to have*. So the past participle of *walk* is *walked* (past perfect: I had walked).

But do not be fooled into thinking that all verbs ending in *-ing* are present participles. It could be that you're facing the dreaded *gerund* form.

A *gerund* is a verb that is turned into a noun by adding *-ing* to its end. Using *walk* as our base verb, *walking* can be both a participle and a gerund. To be sure of which it is, look at the context. If it's operating as a verb or adjective (e.g. *We are walking* or *walking boots*), it's a participle. If it's working as a noun (e.g. *Walking is my favourite pastime*), it's a gerund.

Exercise 29

Using each of the words at the top of this exercise only once, complete the following sentences with a suitable participle or gerund, and then indicate whether you've used a present or past participle or a gerund. Use a separate sheet of paper to note down your answers.

buy   *dance*   *drive*   *enchant*   *give*   *read*   *sense*
speculate   *touch*

1) _____ the tourists were lost, the man offered directions.

2) _____ in Italy can be a stressful activity.

3) _____ by their generosity, he opened the present with a tear in his eye.

4) By _____ astutely, the stock broker made a fortune.

5) _____ the newspaper report, the full horror of the situation struck her.

6) _____ to charity filled Mr Scrooge with a warm glow.

7) He tucked into the feast made with ingredients _____ from the local market.

8) The ballerina spun across the stage, _____ the audience.

9) She dreamed of _____ for the Bolshoi Ballet.

FULL MARKS: PUNCTUATION

Letters make words and words make sentences, but we'd struggle to make much sense of them if it weren't for punctuation. These little symbols help us to structure written language and give clues as to how to interpret meaning. Consider the following pair of sentences:

- I am wrong.

- I am wrong?

The first is an admission of wrongness. The second is a question that may be read as a suggestion of self-doubt by the speaker or perhaps as a challenge to anyone who dares question the speaker's conclusion. Used in conjunction with a consideration of context, punctuation can give vastly different meaning to the same few simple words. Here's a table of the most common punctuation marks and how they're used.

.	Full stop	Denotes the end of a standard sentence.
?	Question mark	Denotes a direct question.
!	Exclamation mark	An alternative to the full stop. Used to grab the reader's attention or to denote a sentence with particularly strong emotion.
-	Hyphen	Used either to conveniently break a long word at the end of a line of text or to link two words together.
"	Quotation marks	Denotes direct speech.
:	Colon	Denotes that the proceeding text summarizes or explains the preceding part of the text.
;	Semi-colon	Used to join two or more independent clauses that don't really deserve to be sentences in themselves.
,	Comma	Denotes a pause or a separate clause within a sentence.

'	Apostrophe	Denotes either possession or the contraction of two words (when it's used in the place of omitted letters – just like I did when I turned 'it is' into 'it's').
–	Dash	Used either alone or as one of a pair (in place of parentheses) to introduce an aside, an interruption or a new piece of information, to indicate a sudden change of emotion or thought, or to show the omission of words.

Comma Again

Of all punctuation, the humble comma and apostrophe in particular come in for prodigious misunderstanding, so let's consider them in a little more detail. To start with, it's worth pointing out that neither is scary – as with all grammar, they're there to make life simpler, not more troublesome!

The comma has a great many uses. Below is a list of the places you might expect to see one:

- Where you wish a reader to pause.

- After introductory words or phrases that come before a main clause.

- Between separate clauses within a sentence.

- Before direct speech.

- In addresses and place names where one part of the place name furnishes information about the other.

- Around non-restrictive phrases.

- After items in a list.

- In large numbers, after every third digit (reading from right to left).

- Before and after an appositive (that's a word or phrase that defines or modifies a noun or pronoun that precedes it).

- After a dependent clause that comes before an independent one.

- After consecutive adjectives.

- Before certain conjunctions linking independent clauses.

- In place of a deliberately omitted word under certain circumstances.

- Before *too* when it is used in the sense of *also*.

- To emphasize certain adverbs.

- After greetings and sign-offs in letters.

As if that weren't enough to take in, British and American English use commas slightly differently. Americans favour the *Oxford comma*, which is a comma before the final *and, or* or *nor* in a list of two or more elements. In Britain, this final comma is not generally used unless it eliminates obvious ambiguity.

In Your Possession

The apostrophe, meanwhile, is a relatively simple language tool made complicated by what at times seems like wilful misuse. It need only be used in two main contexts:

- To replace a letter/letters removed from a contracted word or phrase.
  - e.g. You should not forget the apostrophe in shouldn't!

- To indicate the possessive (before the 's' in a singular noun, after the 's' in a plural and not at all with pronouns).
  - The *President's* official residence is the White House.
  - He has many advisors. When formulating policy, he will listen to these *advisors'* opinions.
  - Ultimately, it is *his* job to sign off legislation.

In Quotes

Quotation marks (or 'inverted commas') also have the propensity to confuse otherwise highly competent writers of English. Used to indicate direct speech, quotations, titles and sometimes even irony (e.g. For a 'bijoux apartment', the flat was both grotty and small), they are governed by few strict rules. Furthermore, just as British and American English use commas differently, so too with quotation marks. For example, it's almost a matter of personal taste as to whether you use single or double quotations (though in the UK it's perhaps more usual to use single ones for primary quotes and double for any further material to be quoted within a quotation, with the reverse the case in the US). As for the question of whether punctuation at the end of the sentence should be inside or outside the inverted commas, the nuances are even subtler. This author, however, favours such punctuation inside the mark if it completes a full sentence that began inside the first quotation mark but outside otherwise. Here goes:

- The boy said he was 'glad to be here'.

   but

- The boy said, 'I'm glad to be here.'

A Useful Tool

Finally, let's take a look at the multi-purpose hyphen. Sometimes it's used to divide a word too long to fit comfortably at the end of a line of text. But if inserted between two separate words it suggests a particularly close relationship between the two, particularly if the two words form a single modifier (e.g. The film star was a well-known womanizer).

So how worried should we be about hyphens in the modern world? Sometimes we can get away with omitting them if the meaning of a sentence remains clear. For example, the following sentence should be hyphenated thus:

- I have collected stamps since I was an eight-year-old.

That said, even without hyphens it is quite clear what the line is saying, but consider these two lines:

- Thirty-odd people belonged to the stamp collectors' society.

- Thirty odd people belonged to the stamp collectors' society.

The first sentence suggests a membership of around thirty people. The second implies a membership of thirty people, all of whom are a bit strange! This is an object lesson in considered use of the hyphen.

Exercise 30

So after all that it's time to put all of this punctuation knowledge to the test.

1) The following lines need to be punctuated. Use whichever symbols you think are required. Write your answers down on a separate sheet of paper.
    a) Do you have a car
    b) My favourite authors are Dickens Hardy and Waugh
    c) A pessimist sees the difficulty in every opportunity an optimist sees the opportunity in every difficulty
    d) She wanted three things from the shop eggs bread and butter
    e) Go away You are not welcome

2) Study the following sentences and decide if the apostrophes in each case are being properly used. If they're not, correct them and add any that you think are missing.

a) I mustnt forget to take my packed lunch.

b) It's a dog's life!

c) Virtue is it's own reward.

d) Have you read all of Sophocles's work?

e) One man was responsible for washing all the player's kits.

f) She loved to watch dancers and owned all of Fred's and Ginger's movies.

3) These sentences are in desperate need of commas. Can you supply them?

a) Having just left the salon I felt like a film star!

b) In November 1918 the First World War finally came to an end.

c) Picasso the famous artist came from Spain.

d) His favourite films were *The Godfather Rocky* and *Sleepless in Seattle*.

e) The house had been abandoned its windows smashed.

4) In each of the following sentences, there's an obvious misuse of quotation marks. Correct each sentence accordingly.

a) 'I'm rich!' he screamed. I've won the lottery.

b) The witness told the judge, 'I heard the defendant demand Open the safe.'

c)   He said 'he'd be home in twenty minutes'.

5) Look at the following three pairs of sentences. Insert hyphens where they are required.

a)   He works on the thirty second floor.
It was a forty four floor office block.

b)   We went on holiday for two weeks.
It was the first two week holiday we'd had in years.

c)   He writes with his right hand.
He is right handed.

FILLING IN THE DETAIL: ADJECTIVES

Adjectives are those words that describe nouns and pronouns. They might tell us, for example, how big something is, its colour, shape, where it's from, and any number of other characteristics.

A few derive from proper nouns to describe historical periods, artistic styles, nationality, geographical locations, philosophical outlooks and much more. Hence we might talk about Dickensian London, the Elizabethan era or Kafkaesque bureaucracies.

There are also *possessive adjectives*, which identify to whom a given noun belongs. They are *my, your, his, her, its, our* and *their*. Please note they're dangerously close in appearance to possessive pronouns, so be careful not to confuse the two.

One Step Further: Adverbs

Adverbs add further meaning to verbs, adjectives and even other adverbs. They can also help answer questions such as *how, when, where, how much* and *how often?* (e.g. How often do you come here? Regularly.) The *-ly* ending can be a clue that we are dealing with an adverb (e.g. beautifully, cleverly), though by no means do all adverbs take this ending (e.g. *hard, often*).

A few words can act as both adverb and adjective. *Early* is an example of just such a word:

- He caught the early train.

- He arrived early for work.

In the first example, *early* is an adjective, since it describes the train. In the second example it's an adverb, since it is modifying the verb *to arrive*.

Exercise 31

For each of the following sentences, note down on a separate sheet of paper any adjectives or adverbs.

1) She wore a blue dress.
2) The awesome landscape opened up before them.
3) The winning team paraded triumphantly round the town.
4) The Inca Empire prospered in pre-Columbian America.
5) She liked nothing more than fast cars.
6) For a big man, he could run fast.
7) The upset customer ranted furiously.
8) Isambard Kingdom Brunel was the greatest engineer of the Victorian era.

More or Less

Comparatives are special sorts of adjective or adverb that, as the name suggests, compare two things. So, a giraffe is *taller* than a mouse, and Albert Einstein was *cleverer* than, well, pretty much everybody.

To form a regular comparative, it's most often a simple case of adding *-er* to the end of the appropriate adjective or adverb (that is to say, *tall* becomes *taller* and *clever* becomes *cleverer*). However, many irregular adjectives or adverbs don't change their ending at all but instead have *more* added in front of them. So, a rose is *beautiful*, but you are *more beautiful*. And if we want to say something is lesser, we always add *less* before the adjective or adverb. Of course, there are some more oddities too. Take *good*, for instance, which becomes *better*.

The *superlative*, meanwhile, is used to describe a subject as imbued with a particular characteristic to the highest degree. To form it with a regular adjective or adverb, add *-est* to the end of the word. So, the giraffe is the *tallest* of all the animals, and Einstein the *cleverest* of all men. With irregular examples, add *most* before the word. Hence, a rose is beautiful, you are more beautiful but Helen of Troy was the most beautiful. And should you be mean enough to be describing someone or something as the *least* example, simply add *least* instead of *most*.

There are a few really irregular comparatives and superlatives but, fortunately, they are a small enough group to be learned off by heart quite easily. Some of the most important are:

	Comparative	**Superlative**
Good	better	best
Bad	worse	worst
Little	less	least
Much	more	most
Far	further/farther	furthest/farthest

Exercise 32

Complete the following sentences with the most appropriate comparative or superlative, using each of the words in the list provided only once. Write your answers down on a separate sheet of paper.

bad   *common*   *funny*   *good*

happy   *mean*   *popular*   *populous*

1) Ebenezer Scrooge was tight with his money but my Uncle Fred is _____.

2) Diamonds are a girl's _____ friend.

3) After she bit all the girls in her class, Nasty Nancy was the _____ girl in her class.

4) The first comedian was amusing but the second one was _____.

5) That zombie kung-fu rom-com was the _____ film I have ever seen.

6) Many foxes live in the city but badgers are _____.

7) My dog doesn't mind running around our garden but when he's running on the beach he is _____.

8) China is the _____ country in the world.

Say It Like You Mean It

Intensifiers are words that add impact to an adverb, adjective or verb. Here are some of the most commonly used:

- Absolutely

- Awfully

- Bitterly

- Dangerously

- Dreadfully

- Easily

- Exceptionally

- Extremely

- Highly

- Moderately

- Much

- Quite

- Really

- Remarkably

- Seriously

- So

- Terribly

- Very

Exercise 33

Decide which of the suggested intensifiers best completes each sentence.

1) He was kept in intensive care because he was
   _____ ill with malaria. (dreadfully/quite)

2) After three weeks of snow, it was still _____ cold
   outside. (moderately/bitterly)

3) She is an _____ talented actor. (so/exceptionally)

4) The movie was not great but was _____
   diverting. (easily/moderately)

ROUNDING OFF: IT ALL COMES TOGETHER

This last section looks at putting everything together, tidying up any last ends and teaching you how to construct a well-written sentence. And there's a little spelling test at the end, too ...

Shall I Compare Thee ...

Similes and *metaphors* are poetic devices allowing you to compare two things with similar characteristics. Almost always, a simile is introduced by either *like* or *as*:

- Her eyes shimmered like the stars.

- He was as sly as a fox.

Metaphors don't have signal words but make a comparison by linking two usually disparate things. One of literature's most famous metaphors is Shakespeare's 'All the world's a stage', creating a connection between the world and the theatre and, later on in the speech, people and actors.

Exercise 34

Below are eight similes and metaphors. Can you complete sentences 1–8 with the suitable phrase from a) to h)?

1) She arrived at the office early, making herself as

   _____.

2) The widower was lost in a _____.

3) He overcame his foe with _____.

4) He approached the situation like _____.

5) The boxer was as _____.

6) He strutted around in his new suit, as

   _____.

7) It was raining _____.

8) The rumours planted _____ in her mind.

   a) steely determination
   b) hard as nails

c)   cats and dogs

d)   sea of grief

e)   seeds of doubt

f)   busy as a bee

g)   proud as a peacock

h)   a bull in a china shop

Join Me

Conjunctions are those words or short phrases that link two other words, phrases, clauses or sentences. There are four chief types:

- *Coordinating conjunctions* – join two sentences (or at least parts of sentences) of equal importance. To remember them, think FANBOYS (*for, and, nor, but, or, yet, so*).

- *Subordinating conjunctions* – link a main clause to a subordinate clause (e.g. *because, although*).

- *Compound conjunctions* – short phrases typically ending in *as* or *that* (e.g. *as long as . . .* and *so that . . .*).

- *Correlative conjunctions* – which work in partnership with other conjunctions (e.g. *either . . . or . . .* and *not only . . . but also . . .*)

Exercise 35

Complete the following sentences using each of the listed conjunctions just once.

and   as soon as   because   but   neither ... nor ...   not
only ... but also ...   so that

1)   He was both a talented singer _____ an adept composer.
2)   He phoned the talking clock _____ he would know the exact time.
3)   She might have been old _____ she wasn't very wise.
4)   _____ Romeo _____ Juliet lived a long life.
5)   He was given a bravery award _____ he helped to catch a thief.
6)   He ordered from the menu _____ he arrived at the restaurant.
7)   He _____ bought all the ingredients _____ baked the cake.

A Time and a Place for Everything

Prepositions help us to locate a noun or pronoun in time or space. Those that place something in time are called *temporal prepositions* and include: *after, before, between, by, during, following, for, from, on, since, till, to, until, within, while* and *except*.

Spatial prepositions, meanwhile, locate their subjects in space, and include: *aboard, about, above, across, against, ahead, along, alongside, amid, amidst, among, amongst, apart, around, aside, astride, at, away, behind, below, beneath, beside, between, beyond, by, close, to, down, in, in between, inside, into, near, next to, on, onto, opposite, out, outside, over, round, through, together, toward, under, underneath, up* and *within*.

Exercise 36

Complete the following sentences using each of the listed prepositions just once.

after   among   behind   beneath   except   from   opposite
since   through   towards   until

1) I have not had a party _____ I was 21.
2) Will you sit in the seat _____ me?
3) I am available every day _____ Tuesday.
4) The skiers drove off _____ the mountains.
5) They were picnicking _____ the branches of a shady tree.
6) Can you give me a call _____ 7 p.m.
7) I could not spot her _____ the crowd of faces.
8) We will be on holiday _____ June _____ July.
9) The cat came in _____ the cat-flap.
10) Meet me in the pub _____ the park.

Everything in Order

To state the obvious, a sentence is a sequence of words that can stand alone to make a statement, ask a question or give a command. Sentences start with a capital letter and usually end with a full stop, question mark or exclamation mark (with odd exceptions, as when an ellipsis is used). They also have a subject and a predicate, which is the part of a sentence made up of a verb and any objects or phrases governed by the verb. A 'sentence' without both subject and verb, which relies on the context of other sentences to convey their meaning, is known as a *fragment*.

We have four main sentence structures, dependent on the number of clauses (distinct parts of a sentence containing a subject and a finite verb):

- The *simple sentence*, consisting of a single clause (e.g. I am learning about sentences).

- The *compound sentence*, consisting of two or more independent clauses, usually joined by a coordinating conjunction (e.g. I am learning about sentences and he is learning about punctuation).

- *Complex sentences*, which have main clauses and subordinate clauses (e.g. Despite being short of time, I like to read a lot). In the example given, 'I like to read a lot' is the main clause, since it is the one that can stand alone.

- *Compound-complex sentences*, consisting of multiple clauses (e.g. When staring to read, which is something most of us do in childhood, we will learn the basics of grammar, along with a great many other skills, at school and also from our parents).

A *relative clause* is one introduced by a relative pronoun. It may be either:

- *Restrictive*, defining something in the main clause and essential to making sense of the sentence.

○ The teacher *who introduced me to Milton* continues to influence me.

- *Non-restrictive* clauses, which add extra information but are not essential.

  ○ My English teacher, *who had studied at Oxford*, was the biggest influence on me.

A *phrase*, meanwhile, is a group of two or more words that are not constructed round a verb but which act together as a single unit in terms of meaning and grammar. These include:

- *Noun phrases* – assuming the role of a noun, as subject, direct object or the object of a preposition.

- *Verb phrases* – any group of words that follows a subject.

- *Adjectival phrases* – which act like an adjective to qualify, or modify, a noun.

- *Adverbial phrases* – which act like an adverb to qualify, or modify, a verb.

- *Prepositional phrases* – consisting of a preposition plus a noun or noun phrase.

Exercise 37

1) Read the following three sentences and mark whether each is simple, compound or complex.

   a) Having set the alarm especially early, she was still late for work.

   b) Because of the fire alarm, we were evacuated from the building.

   c) We wanted to go to the cinema so I phoned up the babysitter.

2) Read the following sentences and mark whether each highlighted clause is restrictive or non-restrictive.

   a) A lion <u>that has been cornered</u> is a dangerous beast.

   b) The lion, <u>which had been trained in a circus</u>, stood on the chair.

   c) The lion-tamer, <u>who had over fifty years of experience</u>, was attacked by a performing armadillo.

3) Look at the highlighted phrases in the following sentences. There are examples of each of the five phrase types but which is which?

   a) I'll see you later <u>at the cinema</u>.

   b) We are going to see <u>a film about cowboys fighting aliens</u>.

   c) The dog <u>chased after the ball</u>.

   d) The puppy was <u>exceptionally cute</u>.

   e) She quit her job <u>quite suddenly</u>.

A Cat in Pyjamas

A modifier describing a noun should be placed as close as possible to its related noun to avoid confusion or ambiguity. Consider the following two sentences:

- A woman was stroking her cat *in pyjamas*.

- A woman *in pyjamas* was stroking her cat.

The *misplaced modifier* ('in pyjamas') means that in the first statement, the cat seems to be wearing nightclothes. The second statement makes it much clearer that the woman was wearing this attire.

Be particularly aware of *dangling participles* such as:

- While cleaning the windows, the ladder gave way.

This statement suggests the ladder was cleaning the window – a clearly ridiculous notion. This confusion wouldn't exist if the sentence were rewritten as:

- While Bob was cleaning the windows, the ladder gave way.

Exercise 38

The following statements all contain a misplaced modifier. Re-write them to remove any ambiguity.

1) Sitting on the train, the book engrossed Fred.
2) He drove a bus wearing slippers.
3) Dave goes back to the hospital where he was born often.

4) He was fined for selling tomatoes to customers that had started to rot.

Before and After

A *prefix* is a group of letters added at the start of a word to modify its meaning. Here are some of the most widely used prefixes, along with their definitions:

Prefix	Meaning
a-/an-/in-/un-/non-	not
ab-	away, from
ad-	movement to, change into, increase
anti-/counter-	opposing, against, the opposite
dis-	negation, removal, expulsion
extra-	outside
hemi-/semi-	half
hyper-	more than, more than normal
inter-	between, among
intra-	inside, within
over-	excessively, completely
post-	after in time or order
pre-/ante-	before, preceding
pro-	favouring, in support of

re–	again
sub–	at a lower position
trans–	across
ultra–	beyond

A *suffix* is a letter or groups of letters added at the end of a word to create a new word. Suffixes come in two main types:

- *Inflectional suffixes*, which don't actually change the meaning of a word but might, for example, conjugate a verb or make a noun plural. So –*s* is a suffix used to create plurals, while –*ed* is a suffix that can denote the past tense.

- *Derivational suffixes*, which do change the meaning of a word, though the meaning remains related to that of the stem word. They can also change one part of speech into another. For example, the addition of –*ly* can change an adjective into an adverb (e.g. *quick* to *quickly*) while an –*ize* can change a noun into a verb (e.g. *atom* to *atomize*). When adding a suffix to a word ending in a consonant followed by a *y*, the *y* generally changes to an *i*, while if the word ends in an *e*, the *e* is usually got rid of.

Exercise 39

1) Rewrite the following six statements, adding a prefix to each highlighted word so that the sentence makes good sense.
   a) Being rude to people is a sure way to become *popular*.
   b) The racers ran round the track *clockwise*.

    c)   She had no interest in matters of government. She was completely *political*.

    d)   The teammates agreed to go for a *match* dinner.

    e)   All sorts of things went on at the nightclub. It was a quite *reputable* place.

    f)   A member of all sorts of clubs, he was always busy with *curricular* activities.

2)   Use each of the available suffixes only once to turn the words listed into new nouns.

-er   -ion   -ment   -ness   -y

Old noun		**New noun**
a)	Teach	_____
b)	Gracious	_____
c)	Master	_____
d)	Collect	_____
e)	Conceal	_____

3)   This time, use each of the available suffixes only once to turn the nouns listed into related adjectives.

-able   -al   -ary   -ful   -ly

Noun	Adjective
a) Nation	_____
b) Friend	_____
c) Fancy	_____
d) Legend	_____
e) Debate	_____

I Shall Say This Only Once

Tautology is the term for an erroneous mistake in which two or more words with the same meaning are used unnecessarily – as in the case of 'erroneous mistake' just now (for what sort of mistake is there other than an erroneous one?).

Exercise 40

Can you spot the tautological phrase in each of the following sentences?

1) Each of the guests at the awards ceremony received a free gift and a complimentary glass of champagne.
2) He was normally quite sensible, but he felt like a stupid idiot when he saw the results of his actions.
3) She loved jewellery and adored the diamond ring he gave her, which was very unique.
4) In an attempt to achieve better quarterly results, the board of directors met to discuss a variety of different ideas.
5) The naughty schoolboy insisted he was telling the honest truth about the smashed window.

I Before E

By common consent, English is a complex language to learn and rules on spelling in particular are few and far between, and subject to numerous exceptions where they do exist. For example, we're taught 'i before e except after c', and could just as easily add 'and except in the case of such common words as height, neighbour, weight and weird!' The harsh truth is that the mastery of spelling comes only through practice.

So, without further ado, I'm going to put your raw talents to the test. After all that grammar this should be a piece (or should that be peice?) of cake …

Exercise 41

Here are twenty-one words that regularly cause confusion. In each case, mark the spelling that's correct. Make a note of the correct spelling on a separate sheet of paper.

	Column A	Column B
1)	accomodate	accommodate
2)	accross	across
3)	achieve	acheive
4)	apparantly	apparently
5)	assasination	assassination
6)	committee	comittee
7)	conscious	concsious
8)	definately	definitely

9)	disappear	dissappear
10)	embarass	embarrass
11)	immediately	imediately
12)	independant	independent
13)	liason	liaison
14)	necessary	neccessary
15)	occasion	occassion
16)	ocurrance	occurrence
17)	possesion	possession
18)	psychology	physcology
19)	rhythm	rythmn
20)	seperate	separate
21)	successful	succesful

Exercise 42

Very well done – we're nearly there! Let's finish our grammar section with a quiz on commonly confused words. Below are pairs of sentences. Work out which of the words in parentheses finishes each sentence.

1) (practice/practise)
   a) The more you _____, the better you'll get.
   b) The doctor ran his own _____.

2) (aloud/allowed)
   a) The trick was ruined when the audience member said _____ the card he was thinking of.

b)   No dogs are _____ on the beach.

3)   (pale/pail)
   a)   A _____ is useful for collecting water.
   b)   When he saw the price of the meal, he went quite

   _____.

4)   (plane/plain)
   a)   The general surveyed his troops, spread out across the

   _____.

   b)   When she flies, she likes to sit in the front part of the

   _____.

5)   (there/their)
   a)   Do you know the people over _____?
   b)   Do you know if _____ friends are also
        coming?

6)   (accept/except)
   a)   I like all vegetables _____ celery.
   b)   I was nervous to join a new team but the other players
        seemed to _____ me.

7)   (lose/loose)
   a)   Make sure your wedding ring is not too

   _____.

   b)   You wouldn't want to _____ it.

8) (stationary/stationery)

   a) The traffic was _____ on the motorway.

   b) A prodigious letter-writer, he always bought good
       _____.

9) (affect/effect)

   a) The training classes had no _____ on the
       naughty dog.

   b) Did the sad film _____ you at all?

WRITTEN IN INK
HANDWRITING

If all that stuff about commas, prepositions and gerunds hasn't put your tail in a spin, it's time now to turn your attention to handwriting. Indeed, having mastered the art of good ol' proper English, it's beholden upon you to present your words elegantly. Even if electronic correspondence is taking over the world, penmanship remains a skill worth spending time developing.

Once you've mastered the basics of the block letter alphabet, it's time to perfect cursive (or joined-up) handwriting. The aim of cursive handwriting is to join up the letters within a word with a flowing script that not only looks neat and attractive, but also allows the author to write more quickly. Take a look at the cursive alphabet:

a b c d e f g h i j k

l m n o p q r s t

u v w x y z . , ? " " !

A B C D E F G H I

J K L M N O P Q R

S T U V W X Y Z

1 2 3 4 5 6 7 8 9 10

On a sheet of lined paper, copy out the cursive alphabet to test your skills. Looks pretty, eh?

Once you've mastered the basics, you can have a go at writing your name. As ever, practice makes perfect, so keep trying until you've mastered it.

Once you've got the hang of each letter you can have a go at writing sentences. There are certain sentences, known as pangrams, which contain all the letters of the alphabet. These are perfect for developing your cursive skills. Perhaps the most famous is:

The quick brown fox jumps over the lazy dog.

This is how it should look:

The quick brown fox jumps over the lazy dog.

Try practising with these other pangrams:

A mad boxer shot a quick, gloved jab to the jaw of his dizzy opponent.

Here's how that one should look:

A mad boxer shot a quick, gloved jab to the jaw of his dizzy opponent.

Here are some other pangrams for you to try:

- Forsaking monastic tradition, twelve jovial friars gave up their vocation for a questionable existence on the flying trapeze.

- The public was amazed to view the quickness and dexterity of the juggler.

- While making deep excavations we found some quaint bronze jewellery.

If ever you lose patience or interest in improving your handwriting, remember that a heart-felt letter copied out in beautiful script is a lot more winning than a text or email will ever be, so go get those stamps and get writing!

SECTION III
ARITHMETIC

Put down your calculators and lock away your protractors, because in this section we go right back to basics. Maths is pretty essential in everyday life, yet if someone were to ask you how you'd tackle a long division question, or how you might convert a fraction into a percentage, chances are you wouldn't have the foggiest. So, sit back, relax and welcome to the surprisingly fun world of maths. Why not turn the page and find out yourself ...

YOUR NUMBER'S UP
MATHEMATICS

From totting up the grocery receipt to dividing up a restaurant bill, basic arithmetic plays an essential role in day-to-day life. It's time now to master the nitty gritty of numbers.

Arithmetic is the branch of maths concerned with the computation of figures. If you can add it, subtract it, divide it or multiply it, you're in the right realm. We all use arithmetic every day, whether it's to tell the time, settle a bill or divide up a pizza for dinner. Let's make a start by looking at a few of those peculiar symbols that form the basis of the language of mathematics:

Symbol	Denoting
+	plus
–	minus
×	multiply by
÷	divide by
=	equals
≠	does not equal
≈	is approximately equal to
<	is less than
>	is greater than
≤	is less than or equal to
≥	is greater than or equal to
√	square root
π	pi (used in numerous calculations related to circles)

BACK TO BASICS: THE CORE MATHEMATICAL PROCESSES

Let's start with something easy to warm things up. You should be able to tackle these sorts of simple mathematical teasers in your head.

It All Adds Up

Try these four quick teasers to get your brain in gear. Whether it's *addition* (+) – the process of adding something to something else, *subtraction* (-) – the process of taking something away from something else, *multiplication* (x) – the process of adding a number to itself a specified number of times, or *division* (÷) – the process of splitting a larger number into an equal number of smaller parts, these tests should remind you how it's done.

Exercise 1

Don't forget to write your answers on a separate sheet of paper.

1)   9 + 6 = ?
2)   27 + 46 = ?
3)   ? + 15 = 32
4)   53 + ? = 91

Exercise 2

1)   12 - 7 = ?
2)   31 - 12 = ?

3)   ? – 14 = 23

4)   95 – ? = 49

Exercise 3

1)   6 x 8 = ?

2)   9 x 14 = ?

3)   ? x 12 = 84

4)   13 x ? = 286

Exercise 4

1)   16 ÷ 4 = ?

2)   70 ÷ 14 = ?

3)   ? ÷ 9 = 12

4)   169 ÷ ? = 13

Top Table

Remember the days of learning your times tables off by heart? Traditionally taught at school for the numbers 1 to 12, times tables provide a great basis for mental arithmetic. In case you can't remember your 7 x 9, or your 12 times table isn't all that it should be, overleaf is a grid that you can use as a reference tool. If you want to check what 7 x 9 is, simply go to column 7 at the top of the table, then move down to the ninth row, and there you'll find the answer.

	1	2	3	4	5	6	7	8	9	10	11	12
1	1	2	3	4	5	6	7	8	9	10	11	12
2	2	4	6	8	10	12	14	16	18	20	22	24
3	3	6	9	12	15	18	21	24	27	30	33	36
4	4	8	12	16	20	24	28	32	36	40	44	48
5	5	10	15	20	25	30	35	40	45	50	55	60
6	6	12	18	24	30	36	42	48	54	60	66	72
7	7	14	21	28	35	42	49	56	63	70	77	84
8	8	16	24	32	40	48	56	64	72	80	88	96
9	9	18	27	36	45	54	63	72	81	90	99	108
10	10	20	30	40	50	60	70	80	90	100	110	120
11	11	22	33	44	55	66	77	88	99	110	121	132
12	12	24	36	48	60	72	84	96	108	120	132	144

Here are a few useful tricks to help you master multiplication:

- For numbers in the 2 times table, you're simply doubling (e.g. 2 x 3 = 6).

- For numbers in the 4 times table, you're doubling twice (e.g. 4 x 3 = double double 3 = double 6 = 12).

- For numbers in the 8 times table, you're doubling three times (e.g. 8 x 3 = double double double 3 = double double 6 = double 12 = 24).

- For numbers in the 5 times table, multiply by 10 and then halve the result (e.g. for 5 x 3, calculate 10 x 3 [which is 30] and then halve it to make 30 ÷ 2 = 15).

- For numbers in the 10 times table, add a 0 (e.g. 10 x 7 = 70).

- In the 11 times table, simply repeat the number you're multiplying by for figures up to 9 (e.g. 11 x 3 = 33). We know how to calculate 10 x 11 (see above), but 11 x 11 and 12 x 11 you'll just need to learn by heart.

- For the 9 times table, you can use your hands for figures up to 10. Put both hands out in front of you and from the left, count to the finger that represents the number of nines you want (so for 3 x 9, count to the middle finger of your left hand). Fold that finger down. This leaves 2 fingers before it and 7 – including thumbs – after it, so 3 x 9 = 27. We know how to work out 9 x 11 from the 11 times table rule above, which means you only need to memorize 12 x 9.

- It sometimes helps to rearrange a division sum into a multiplication one. Hence, 35 ÷ 5 = ? can be rephrased as ? x 5 = 35. Basic knowledge of the times tables reveals the answer to be 7.

Exercise 5

Copy the grid overleaf onto a separate sheet of paper and replace each question mark with a number so that each calculation across and down gives the answer shown in bold. Each number from 1 to 9 appears in the grid once. Calculations should be performed from left to right and from top to bottom.

?	+	8	–	2	**11**
x		x		–	
?	÷	?	x	?	**18**
–		–		+	
?	–	?	x	4	**24**
23		**23**		**-3**	

Exercise 6

Now try these teasers to further test your mental arithmetic capabilities.

1) Tom gets on a train to Clapham Junction at 10.09. His journey should take 38 minutes. At what time will he arrive?

2) Kieran pays for a bag of crisps with a 50 pence piece. The bag costs 28 pence. How much money will he get back?

3) Lewis drives at an average speed of 40 miles per hour. How much distance will he cover in 2 ½ hours?

4) Lewis' friend, Jenson, covered 720 km over the course of 8 hours. What was his average distance covered per hour?

5) Jo is buying sandwiches for lunch for herself and three colleagues. She has taken £10 from petty cash. Each sandwich costs £1.85. How much change will she get?

6) Lewis and Jenson went on a road trip. They drove an average of 56 km per hour for 12 hours. If they can travel

an average of 48 km per gallon of fuel, how many gallons will they use?

PLUSES AND MINUSES: NEGATIVE NUMBERS

Most of us deal in positive numbers in everyday life. However, sometimes we'll encounter *negative numbers*, which is to say a figure with a value less than 0, indicated by a minus symbol preceding it. These are, strictly speaking, part of pure maths rather than applied maths. This is because they're theoretical rather than actual – just try making -1 cups of tea. Nonetheless, negative numbers are of great practical use. Without them, for example, bank statements would be utter gibberish. Although, maybe that's not such a bad thing . . .

Get In Line

Initially, learning to calculate with negative numbers can be confusing because adding a negative number is like subtracting a positive one. The following calculations show how negative numbers affect a series of ostensibly simple sums:

- $2 + 3 = 5$

- $-2 + 3 = 1$

- $-2 - 3 = -5$

- $2 - 3 = -1$

- $2 - -3 = 5$

If that all seems bewildering, there's a technique to simplify things. Take a look at this number line:

-7 -6 -5 -4 -3 -2 -1 0 1 2 3 4 5 6 7

- Firstly, make the first number in your sum your starting point. Stand by that number.

- If you're adding, turn to face the higher numbers. If you're subtracting, turn towards the lower ones.

- If the number you're adding or subtracting is positive, carry on in the direction that you're facing. If it's a negative number, walk backwards.

Try calculating 2 - -3 in this way. Stand by 2 on the number line. It's a subtraction, so face the lower numbers. The second figure is negative so reverse 3 spaces. You find yourself at 5, the answer to the sum. With practice, you'll be able to walk the number line in your imagination rather than having to write one out each time.

Exercise 7

Calculate the results of these sums containing a mix of positive and negative numbers.

1) 7 + -5 = ?
2) -4 - 4 = ?
3) -5 + 11 = ?

4)   10 - 16 = ?

5)   -6 - 2 - 3 = ?

6)   -19 + 16 = ?

7)   7 + -9 = ?

8)   -5 + 12 = ?

9)   -5 - 14 = ?

10) -6 - -9 = ?

Two Wrongs Don't Make a Right

It's a rule oft repeated in schools that two negatives don't make a positive. This is a golden rule to remember in arithmetic. Here are some key points to remember when multiplying or dividing with negatives:

- Multiplying a positive number and a negative number gives a negative result.
  - -3 x 5 = -15

- Multiplying two negatives gives a positive result.
  - -3 x -5 = 15

- Dividing a negative number by a positive one gives you a negative but bigger number than the one you started with.
  - -12 ÷ 2 = -6 (-6 being a 'bigger' number than -12)

- Dividing a positive number by a negative number gives you a negative result.
  - 12 ÷ -2 = -6

- Dividing a negative by a negative gives you a positive result.
  - $-12 \div -2 = 6$

In the simplest terms: if you're multiplying or dividing with a mixture of positives and negatives, the result will always be negative. Multiply or divide only with negatives, and the result will be positive.

Exercise 8

Armed with that information, try solving the following sums.

1) $-4 \times 5 = ?$
2) $-8 \times -6 = ?$
3) $-25 \div 5 = ?$
4) $4 \times -17 = ?$
5) $-49 \div -7 = ?$
6) $-24 \times 8 = ?$
7) $192 \div -16 = ?$
8) $-17 \times -17 = ?$

ALL WRITTEN OUT: PAPER ARITHMETIC

However adept at mental arithmetic you become, some sums are simply too complex to do in your head. Instead you'll have to work them out on paper. For paper arithmetic, it's important to understand the principles of column arithmetic, which requires numbers to be lined up under each other with their place values aligned.

To understand place value, you must realize that the value of a figure depends upon the number column in which it appears. In whole numbers, the columns increase in value from right to left. The column at the far right of a whole number represents units (numbers with a value between 0 and 9). The column to its left represents 10s, to the left again are 100s, then 1,000s, 10,000s, 100,000s, 1,000,000s and so on.

Thus if we are presented with the number 5,678, we know that it consists of 8 units, 7 tens (or 70), 6 hundreds (600) and 5 thousands (5,000).

Decimals work slightly differently. The numbers before the point operate just as we've discussed, but the numbers after the decimal read from left to right, with the first column indicating the number of tenths, the column to its right the hundredths, to its right the thousandths and so on. So, in the number 1.234, we know we are dealing with 1 unit, 2 tenths, 3 hundredths and 4 thousandths.

More or Less

Having got to grips with place value, undertaking the basic operations of adding, subtracting, dividing and multiplying is really quite straightforward.

To add two or more numbers using paper arithmetic, put them in a correctly aligned column. Then simply add the numbers in each column (starting at the right and moving to the left), noting the result at the bottom of each column.

So for the sum:

$$\begin{array}{r} 1,\ 2\ \ 3\ \ 4\ _+ \\ 7\ \ 6\ \ 5 \\ \hline \end{array}$$

- First, add the 4 + 5 in the right hand column (= 9).

- Then 3 + 6 in the next one along (= 9).

- Then 2 + 7 (= 9).

- Finally, 1 + 0 (= 1).

$$\begin{array}{r} 1,\ 2\ \ 3\ \ 4\ _+ \\ 7\ \ 6\ \ 5 \\ \hline 1,\ 9\ \ 9\ \ 9 \end{array}$$

However, sometimes the figures in a column will add up to more than 9. In such cases, we start 'carrying' – which means that any 'spare' digit is added into the column to the left. Say you're adding 323 + 89:

$$\begin{array}{r} 3\ \ 2\ \ 3\ _+ \\ 8\ \ 9 \\ \hline \end{array}$$

- Starting in the right hand column, 3 + 9 = 12.

- Put the 2 of the 12 at the bottom of the column and carry the 1 of 12 (in reality, a value of ten) to the 'tens' column to the left. (It's customary to put any carried numbers at the top of the column to remind you to add them.)

- In the middle column, we now need to add 2 + 8 + 1 (the 1 we've carried over). This comes to 11, so put 1 at the bottom of the column and carry the other 1 to the next column on the left.

- In the final column we add the 3 already there to the 1 we've carried over, to give us 4. So the answer is 412:

```
1   1
3   2   3  +
    8   9
_____
4   1   2
```

To subtract on paper, align the number you're subtracting underneath the number you're subtracting from. Just as with addition, start in the column on the right and work leftwards, in each case subtracting the lower figure from the one above it.

For example:

```
1   5   7  −
    3   2
_____
1   2   5
```

However, if the number you're subtracting in a particular column is bigger than the number above it, you will need to 'borrow', which is essentially 'carrying' in reverse.

Take the example 556 - 93:

```
5  5  6 _
      9  3
?  ?  ?
```

• Starting in the far right column, 6 - 3 = 3, so put 3 at the bottom of the column.

• In the next column, we have 5 - 9. Since this equals -4, our sum is going to get in a mess. So we 'borrow' a 1 from the column to the left. Now we have 15 - 9, which of course equals 6. So put this figure into your answer.

• Having borrowed 1 from the 5 in the column to the far left, change the 5 to a 4. This gives a sum of 4 - 0 = 4. So our answer is 463:

```
4̵5̵ ¹5  6 _
      9  3
4  6  3
```

Should you need to borrow from a column with a zero in it, the 0 becomes a 9. However, eventually you will need to borrow from the next number over 0 too, along with any 0s in between. So:

```
2  0  0  6 _
      1  9  7
```

becomes:

```
 21  ¹0̶9  ¹0̶9  ¹4  _
          1    9    7
  1    8    0    7
```

Exercise 9

Now have a go at solving the following problems.

1) Jack saved £36 in April, £45 in May and £73 in June. How much spending money did he have for his holiday in July?

2) Jill took £373 on holiday and spent £179 in the first week. How much did she have left for the second week?

3) Three schools gathered for a giant sports day. School A brought 745 pupils, School B 769 and School C 832. How many pupils were present in total?

4) A crowd of 9,873 fans turned up for a football match. With the score standing at 14-0 at half time, the fans of one of the teams left en masse. 4,898 people went home early. What was the size of the crowd in the second half?

5) The bill for dinner arrived and showed that Des's meal cost £17.89, Kate's cost £21.43 and Kim's cost £15.47. What was the total cost?

6) A business took £3,779.98 in a week of trading. Its costs over that period came to £1,678.54. How much profit did the company make?

Sign of the Times

Multiplication is really just a case of adding, but doing it lots of times. Take the sum 4 x 6, which could equally be expressed as 4 + 4 + 4 + 4 + 4 + 4. We express such sums in terms of multiplication because it's quicker than repeatedly adding.

Multiplication can soon seem overwhelmingly complex, but it needn't be. While 6 x 4 may not be such a hard sum, 6 x 14 can easily set alarm bells ringing. However, we can quickly simplify the sum by treating it as two separate calculations, the results of which are then added together. Remembering place value, 14 is made of 1 in the 'tens' column and 4 in the 'units'. So, we would calculate 6 x 10 (= 60) and 6 x 4 (= 24), to give us an answer of 84.

The same system works with still more challenging sums. If presented with 14 (1 ten and 4 units) x 29 (2 tens and 9 units), divide the sum into 'chunks':

- 10 x 20 = 200

- 4 x 20 = 80

- 10 x 9 = 90

- 4 x 9   = 36

- **Total = 406**

You can even use a grid to make things easier:

	20	**9**
10	10 x 20 = 200	10 x 9 = 90
4	4 x 20 = 80	4 x 9 = 36

Sometimes, though, a multiplication sum might be so involved that even the grid method leaves you with unwieldy calculations. In such cases, use *long multiplication*. As an example, we'll work through the sum 47 x 163:

$$
\begin{array}{ccc}
1 & 6 & 3 \times \\
  & 4 & 7 \\
\hline
\end{array}
$$

- Start on the far right column: 3 x 7 = 21. Put the 1 into your answer at the bottom of the column. The 2 is carried (remember our addition sums?) into the tens column.

- Now, multiply the 6 in the tens column by the 7 then **add** the 2 carried over. This gives 44. So, 4 goes at the bottom of the column and the 4 is carried over.

- Next, multiply the 1 in the hundreds column by the 7 and add the 4 you've carried over. This comes to 11. Since there are no more columns to carry over, put 11 into the answer:

$$
\begin{array}{cccc}
  & {\scriptstyle 4} & {\scriptstyle 2} &   \\
  & 1 & 6 & 3 \times \\
  &   & 4 & 7 \\
\hline
1 & 1 & 4 & 1 \\
\end{array}
$$

- That's the first half of the sum done. Now we go through

the same process, but rather than multiply by the 7 in 47, we multiply by the 4.

- For convenience, strike through the 42 and note any new carried figures above them. Put your answer underneath the 1,141.

- Since the 4 in 47 represent 4 tens, we won't use the units column in the answer, so insert a 0 in this column.

- 4 x 3 = 12. Put the 2 in the tens column and carry 1 over.

- 4 x 6 = 24. Add the carried 1, and you get 25. Put 5 into your answer and carry the 2.

- Finally, 4 x 1 + the 2 carried over = 6. Put this into your answer:

$$
\begin{array}{r}
\overset{2}{}\ \overset{1}{} \\
\overset{4}{}\ \overset{2}{} \\
1\ \ 6\ \ 3\ \times \\
4\ \ 7 \\
\hline
1\ \ 1\ \ 4\ \ 1 \\
6\ \ 5\ \ 2\ \ 0
\end{array}
$$

- Finally, add your two answers together, which comes to 7,661. So 163 x 47 = 7,661.

- Should the figure you're multiplying by have three figures, remember to put 0s in the units and tens columns when multiplying by the figure in the hundreds columns. Add an additional zero for every additional row of results.

Exercise 10

1) Use the grid method to solve the following sums:
   a) $18 \times 9 = ?$
   b) $19 \times 27 = ?$
   c) $112 \times 35 = ?$

2) Use long multiplication to solve the following sums:
   a) $32 \times 147 = ?$
   b) $47 \times 343 = ?$
   c) $117 \times 193 = ?$

3) Use whichever method you require to solve the following problems:
   a) A company employs 17 people, each of whom works an average of 37 hours per week. How many hours per week do the staff work combined?
   b) In one county there are 29 secondary schools with an average of 635 pupils each. How many pupils are there in total?
   c) A rock band toured for 43 years. They played an average of 167 gigs per year, each lasting on average 87 minutes. How many minutes were they on stage for over the duration of their career?

Divide and Conquer

Fun stuff, eh? Now it's time to turn to division. For division sums too complex to do in your head, we set out the calculation on paper a little differently. Consider the example $207 \div 9$.

- Start by writing it out like this:

$$9 \,\overline{|\; 2 \quad 0 \quad 7}$$

- Unlike the other sums we've looked at, work from the left hand column towards the right. 9 doesn't go into 2, so put 0 above the 2 and carry the 2 across to the next column:

$$\begin{array}{c} 0 \\ 9 \,\overline{|\; 2 \quad {}^2 0 \quad 7} \end{array}$$

- 9 goes into 20 twice with 2 left over. So put 2 in your answer and carry the spare 2 into the next column:

$$\begin{array}{c} 0 \quad 2 \\ 9 \,\overline{|\; 2 \quad {}^2 0 \quad {}^2 7} \end{array}$$

- Finally, 9 goes perfectly into 27 three times. So put that 3 into your answer. You can now see that $207 \div 9 = 23$.

$$\begin{array}{c} 0 \quad 2 \quad 3 \\ 9 \,\overline{|\; 2 \quad {}^2 0 \quad {}^2 7} \end{array}$$

Alas, not all division sums are quite so straightforward – often one figure doesn't divide into another quite so neatly, in which case we find we're left with a *remainder* in the final column. If this happens, add a decimal point after the final figure and then a 0. Simply carry on with the calculation, adding more 0s as necessary until the equation works out. For example, if presented with 399 ÷ 6:

$$
\begin{array}{c|cccc}
& 0 & 6 & 6 \cdot & 5 \\
\hline
6 & 3 & {}^{3}9 & {}^{3}9 \cdot & {}^{3}0 \\
\end{array}
$$

So 399 ÷ 6 = 66·5.

Occasionally, though, even this method won't work and you'll find yourself in a recurring loop. An example of just such a sum is 1 ÷ 3:

$$
\begin{array}{c|ccccccccc}
& 0 \cdot & 3 & 3 & 3 & 3 & 3 & 3 & 3 & 3 \\
\hline
3 & 1 \cdot & {}^{1}0 & {}^{1}0 & {}^{1}0 & {}^{1}0 & {}^{1}0 & {}^{1}0 & {}^{1}0 & {}^{1}0 \\
\end{array}
$$

You could keep on adding 0s for evermore but the sum will outlast you. This is called a recurring decimal and it can be simplified by putting a dot over the recurring figure (and if a sequence of numbers recurs, put a dot over the first and last digits). Hence, 1 ÷ 3 = 0.$\dot{3}$.

If your sum is really complex, you can turn to *long division*. Redolent with memories of classroom terror, it's nonetheless a very useful weapon to have in your armoury. Here's how it's done, using 837 ÷ 31 as a sample sum.

Write your problem out as normal:

$$31 \overline{)8 \quad 3 \quad 7}$$

Again, work from the left. 31 doesn't go into 8 so put a 0 over the 8. But it does go into 83 (the first two digits) twice. So put a 2 over the 3 of 83.

$$31 \overline{)8 \quad \overset{2}{3} \quad 7}$$

Now you must remember to multiply the 2 in your answer by the 31, giving 62. Put this figure under the 83.

$$
\begin{array}{r}
2 \\
31 \overline{)8 \quad 3 \quad 7} \\
6 \quad 2
\end{array}
$$

Now subtract the 62 from 83, to give us 21. Write this figure underneath.

$$
\begin{array}{r}
2 \\
31 \overline{)8 \quad 3 \quad 7} \\
\underline{6 \quad 2} \\
2 \quad 1
\end{array}
$$

Next move down the spare 7 from 837 and put it at the end of your 21 to give 217.

```
        2
31 |  8   3   7
      6   2
      2   1   7
```

Does 31 go into 217? Yes, 7 times. Put this 7 into your result at the top of the sum.

```
        2   7
31 |  8   3   7
      6   2
      2   1   7
```

There's no remainder and nothing left to bring down, so the sum is complete. 837 ÷ 31 thus equals 27.

Now it's time to crank up the difficulty. Imagine that your original sum was 8,401 ÷ 31. By following the same steps as above, your sum will get to this stage:

```
        2
31 |  8   4   0   1
      6   2
      2   2   0
```

31 goes into 220 seven times, so put 7 into your answer at the top. 7 x 31 = 217, so subtract 217 from 220, to give you 3. Next, bring down the final 1 in 8,401. Your sum now looks like this:

```
            2   7
    31 │ 8  4   0   1
          6  2
          2  2   0
          2  1   7
                 3   1
```

31 goes into 31 once, so put 1 into your answer at the top:

```
            2   7   1
    31 │ 8  4   0   1
          6  2
          2  2   0
          2  1   7
                 3   1
```

There's no remainder and nothing left to bring down, so the sum is complete. 8,401 ÷ 31 thus equals 271.

Often, the end of a long division sum does not conclude so neatly. In such cases, your answer will end in a decimal. Consider, for instance, the sum 720 ÷ 32. Following the long division steps, we come to this sum:

```
            2   2
    32 │ 7  2   0
          6  4
          8   0
          6   4
          1   6
```

32 doesn't go into 16 neatly, but $32 \div 16 = 0.5$, so .5 must go at the end of your answer:

```
         2   2 · 5
  32 | 7  2   0
       6  4
          8   0
          6   4
          1   6
```

Thus, $720 \div 32 = 22.5$.

Exercise 11

1) Solve the following sums using the short division method. Don't forget to write your answers down on a separate sheet of paper:
   a) $243 \div 9 = ?$
   b) $253 \div 23 = ?$
   c) $126 \div 12 = ?$

2) Now things get a little more tough. Solve the following sums using the long division method:
   a) $481 \div 37 = ?$
   b) $1,034 \div 47 = ?$
   c) $1,053 \div 78 = ?$

3) It's time to mix things up! Use whichever method you require to solve the following problems:

a) Anton spends £558 in January. How much on average does he spend each day?

b) 22 football matches held over the course of one weekend attracted 253,550 spectators. What is the average size of crowd?

c) A syndicate of 34 people wins £42,449 on the lottery. How much does each member receive?

Order, Order

Now you've well and truly mastered the basics, let's take a look at the *order of operations*. Sometimes, you'll be confronted with a conundrum that requires you to carry out a series of different operations. The order in which you undertake them can have a big effect on the answer. Consider what appears to be a straightforward calculation: 7 + 2 x 9 = ?

If we do it in the order that it appears, we get an answer of 81 (7 + 2 = 9; 9 x 9 = 81). But if we do the multiplication bit first (2 x 9 = 18) and then add the 7, we get 25. Fortunately, there are some ground rules to avoid this sort of ambiguity. There's even a handy mnemonic, BIDMAS, to help you remember the order of operations:

- Brackets (i.e. anything that appears in parentheses)

- Indices (see p.152)

- Division

- Multiplication

- Addition

- Subtraction

Exercise 12

Use BIDMAS to solve these problems.

1) $14 + 3^2 - 5 = ?$
2) $18 + 12 \div 4 = ?$
3) $7 \times (8 + 3) - 5 = ?$
4) $5^3 + (6 + 4)^2 = ?$
5) $12 \times 18 \div 3 = ?$

Exercise 13

Each of the following problems is missing brackets. Insert them in the correct place:

1) $10 + 36 \div 6 = 16$
2) $16 - 22 + 5 = -11$
3) $108 \div 3 \times 4 + 16 = 25$
4) $6 \times 22 + 35 \div 5 = 139$

ALL FOUR CORNERS: SQUARE NUMBERS

Indices (singular: index) are a sort of maths shorthand indicating that a number is to be multiplied by itself a specific number of times. Say 4 is to be multiplied by itself and n is the unspecified index, we write 4^n (or alternatively '4 to the power of n' or '4 to the nth power').

To Square or to Cube?

The most common indices you'll encounter are 2 and 3. If a number has an index of 2, it's described as squared and is multiplied by itself once. Hence, 4^2 is equivalent to 4 x 4 (or 16). If the index is 3, a number is described as cubed and is multiplied by itself twice. So 4^3 is equivalent to 4 x 4 x 4 (or 64). As the index gets larger, you can find yourself dealing with very big numbers indeed. For example, 4^9 (or 4 x 4 x 4 x 4 x 4 x 4 x 4 x 4 x 4) = 262,144.

Exercise 14

What are the following values?

1) 4^2
2) 3^3
3) 5^3
4) -6^2
5) 6^3

6) 17^2
7) 20^3

Rooting out the Problem

Just as you can square a number, so you can 'unsquare' it, or, to use the correct terminology, calculate its *square root* (denoted by the symbol $\sqrt{}$). Taking 3 as an example, we know that $3^2 = 9$. Therefore, the square root of 9 = 3 (which we express as $\sqrt{9} = 3$).

In exactly the same way, we can cube root ($\sqrt[3]{}$) a number. So, as we know that $3^3 = 27$, we also know that $\sqrt[3]{27} = 3$.

Exercise 15

Calculate the following.

1) $\sqrt{64}$
2) $\sqrt{256}$
3) $\sqrt[3]{64}$
4) $\sqrt[3]{2,744}$
5) $\sqrt{1,000,000}$
6) $\sqrt[3]{15,625}$

KEEPING THINGS IN PROPORTION: RATIO AND PROPORTION

A *ratio* is a comparison of two numbers, often indicated by the presence of a colon separating them. A *proportion*, on the other hand, is an equation showing two ratios as equal.

Sorry, What's That?

Imagine you're baking a batch of 20 biscuits. The recipe instructs you to add 100 grams of sugar and 50 grams of butter. The ratio of sugar to butter could be described as 100:50, which could be further simplified to 2:1. With this knowledge, you'll always know how much butter and sugar to add no matter the size of batch of biscuits. If you were baking 40 biscuits rather than 20, you would thus need to add 200 grams of sugar and 100 of butter. If you wanted a batch of only 10, you'd use 50 grams of sugar and 25 of butter. That's a ratio.

To understand what a proportion is, imagine two plots of land next to each other. Plot A is 30 metres by 15 metres (a ratio in its simplest terms of 2:1). Plot B is smaller than Plot A but is in the same proportion. We have measured its length as 15 metres but don't know the width. We might present the proportion as $2/1 = 15/?$. Doing a simple bit of arithmetic, we realize that ? (the unknown width) must thus equal 7.5 metres.

Exercise 16

1) In a class of 30, there were 18 boys and 12 girls. What is the ratio of boys to girls in its simplest form?

2) In the school as a whole, the ratio of girls to boys is 8:7. If there are 256 girls in the school, how many boys are there?

3) A football stadium is divided between away supporters and home supporters in the ratio of 2:7. If there are seats for 3,200 away supporters, how many are there for home supporters?

4) When Dave went to get his holiday money, the exchange rate from pounds sterling to euros was 1:0.85. How many euros did he get for his £250?

5) A cocktail especially designed for mathematicians and called a Ratio Fizz calls for a mixture of 120 ml of brandy per 780 ml of orange juice. A tumbler is filled with 130 ml of orange juice. How much brandy should be added?

MATTER OF FACTORS: FACTORIZING

A *factor* is any number that divides exactly into another one. For example, the factors of 4 are 1, 2 and 4. The factors of 6 are 1, 2, 3 and 6.

Tooled Up

Factoring is a useful tool for a mathematician and we will see how it is used in algebra in due course. Factoring is also essential for understanding what a prime number is, more of which anon.

Exercise 17

List all the factors of the following numbers.

1) 3
2) 12
3) 25
4) 16
5) 72

PRIME TIME: PRIME NUMBERS

A *prime number* is a number greater than 1 but divisible only by 1 and itself. There are an infinite number of prime numbers, and 168 of them have a value less than 1,000.

Endless Possibilities

Blessed with a range of particular properties, prime numbers are of endless use to theoretical mathematicians. Yet even for those operating at a more modest level, it's well worth being familiar with them. Being on top of your factoring will help you to recognize those that nestle in the lower end of the range.

Exercise 18

1) In each of the following groups of numbers, only one
   number is prime. Can you identify which one?
   a)   15, 21, 23, 27
   b)   104, 105, 111, 113
   c)   251, 253, 255, 256
   d)   753, 755, 757, 759

2) This time, the groups encompass blocks of prime numbers.
   In each case, can you add the next one in the sequence?
   a)   29, 31, 37, _____
   b)   83, 89, 97, _____
   c)   432, 433, 439, _____
   d)   827, 829, 839, _____

COMPUTER MAD: BINARY NUMBERS

In everyday life, we work with the *decimal system* of numbers (also
known as base-10), comprising the digits 0 to 9. When we need
to talk about numbers larger than 9, we employ a column for
tens, hundreds, thousands etc., but use the same basic digits in
each column. However, it's possible to use other *base numbers*. The
most familiar alternative is base-2 (or *binary*), a system that has
underpinned computer programming for decades.

All the Twos

Binary uses only the digits 0 and 1, with the value of columns ascending by double the value of the previous column (as opposed to 10 times in the decimal system). Compare the first six column values of decimal and binary:

Decimal:	100,000	10,000	1,000	100	10	1
Binary:	32	16	8	4	2	1

- So to express 1 in binary, we would write 1.

- To express 2, we would write 10 (that is 0 in the 1 column and 1 in the 2 column).

- To express 3, we would write 11 (that is 1 in the 1 column + 1 in the 2 column).

- And to express 18, it would be 10010!

But how does binary deal with fractions? The answer, in short, is imperfectly. A great many common fractions cannot be precisely rendered in binary (for example, 0.1 in decimal has no exact binary equivalent). While the figures after a decimal point are worth tenths, hundredths, thousandths etc., in binary they are worth halves, quarters, eighths and so on, as the following shows:

	0.1	0.01	0.001	0.0001	0.00001
Decimal value:	1/10	1/100	1/1.000	1/10,000	1/100,000
Binary value:	1/2	1/4	1/8	1/16	1/32

So, for example, 0.1 in binary is equivalent to ½ or 0.5 in decimal.

Exercise 19

1) Look at the binary numbers below and express them as decimal numbers. Don't forget to write down your answers on a separate sheet of paper.
   a) 101
   b) 1011
   c) 10001
   d) 101010

2) Now try these.
   a) 0.01
   b) 10.11
   c) 1.101

3) Express the following decimal numbers in binary.
   a) 7
   b) 13
   c) 14
   d) 125

Exercise 20

1) Here are some arithmetic questions using binary. Give the answers in binary too.
   a) 1001 + 111 = ?
   b) 10101 - 10 = ?

c)   1000 x 110 = ?

2)   This time, give the answers as decimals.
      a)   101001 + 100000 - 1000 = ?
      b)   1.001 + 1.001 = ?
      c)   1000 x 10.01 = ?

GOOD THINGS COME IN SMALL PACKAGES: FRACTIONS

We've looked at a few non-whole numbers but it's now time to study them in much more depth. Any smaller part of a whole number is called a *fraction*, and for each number there are an infinite number of fractions.

Fractions may be expressed in any one of several forms, including:

- Vulgar fractions

- Decimals

- Percentages

Preaching to the Converted

To truly master fractions, it's necessary to know how to express them in all their forms. Many of these equivalent terms are so familiar that you'll know them off by heart. The following table shows some of the key figures:

Vulgar	Decimal	Percentage
$\frac{1}{100}$	0.01	1%
$\frac{1}{50}$	0.02	2%
$\frac{1}{40}$	0.025	2.5%
$\frac{1}{25}$	0.04	4%
$\frac{1}{20}$	0.05	5%
$\frac{1}{10}$	0.1	10%
$\frac{1}{5}$	0.2	20%
$\frac{1}{4}$	0.25	25%
$\frac{1}{3}$	0.3 recurring	33.3%
$\frac{1}{2}$	0.5	50%
$\frac{2}{3}$	0.6 recurring	66.6%
$\frac{3}{4}$	0.75	75%
$\frac{4}{5}$	0.8	80%
$\frac{1}{1}$	1.0	100%

However, for those conversions that don't come quite so naturally to you, here are some useful rules:

- To convert a decimal into a percentage, multiply the decimal by 100 and add a percentage symbol at the end (e.g. 0.2 = 0.2 x 100 = 20%).

- To convert a percentage into a decimal, remove the percentage sign and divide the figure by 100 (e.g. 20% = 20 ÷ 100 = 0.2).

- To convert a vulgar fraction into a percentage, multiply the fraction by $\frac{100}{1}$ and add a percentage symbol at the end (e.g. $\frac{1}{5}$ = $\frac{1}{5}$ x $\frac{100}{1}$ = $\frac{100}{5}$ = 20 = 20%).

- To convert a percentage into a vulgar fraction, remove the percentage sign and divide the figure by 100 (e.g. 20% = $\frac{20}{100}$ = $\frac{1}{5}$).

- To convert a vulgar fraction into a decimal, treat your vulgar fraction as a simple division.

$$\frac{1}{5} = \frac{0.2}{5 \overline{)1.^10}} = 0.2$$

- To convert a decimal into a vulgar fraction, you need to think in terms of place value. In 0.2, 2 is in the tenths column. So do the following sum: 0.2 = $\frac{2}{10}$ = $\frac{1}{5}$. If you have multiple figures after the decimal it gets trickier. For example, 0.25 = $\frac{2}{10}$ + $\frac{5}{100}$ = $\frac{20}{100}$ + $\frac{5}{100}$ = $\frac{25}{100}$ = $\frac{1}{4}$. If there was a figure in the thousandths column, your lowest common denominator would be 1,000, and so on for every additional figure after the decimal point. Remember always to cancel down your final result too.

How Vulgar!

Vulgar fractions are represented by one number sitting on a line above another. For example, half as a vulgar fraction is $\frac{1}{2}$. The value of a vulgar fraction is equal to the value of the top number (called the *numerator*) divided by the bottom number (the *denominator*).

When calculating with vulgars, there's an invaluable concept called the *equivalence of fractions*. What this really means is that, unlike with whole numbers, a fraction may be represented in myriad ways without changing its fundamental value. So, as an example, all of the following vulgar fractions are equivalent to ½:

- $\frac{2}{4}$ $\frac{3}{6}$ $\frac{4}{8}$ $\frac{5}{10}$ $\frac{16}{32}$ $\frac{79}{158}$

By thinking of each fraction as a division sum (dividing the top number by the bottom number), you get exactly the same value in each case (namely, a half, or 0.5 or ½ or 50%). Another quick trick for simplifying fractions is to divide the numerator and denominator by a value that goes into both numbers equally. (So, for example, 4 divides evenly into $\frac{4}{8}$ to leave ½.)

Exercise 21

1) Rewrite the following values as vulgar fractions:
   a) three-quarters
   b) one-third
   c) five-sixths
   d) seven-tenths

2) Re-write the following equations in their simplest form.
   a) $\frac{32}{48}$
   b) $\frac{125}{200}$
   c) $\frac{15}{40}$
   d) $\frac{72}{90}$

A Bit at a Time

In order to add or subtract vulgar fractions, they must share a common denominator. While we can add or subtract thirds together, we cannot add or subtract a third and a quarter. This is one of the reasons why equivalence of fractions is so important.

In order to calculate with a third and a quarter, we must establish their lowest common denominator. Let's work through an example calculation: $\frac{1}{3} + \frac{1}{4} = ?$

- The denominator of $\frac{1}{3}$ is 3 and of $\frac{1}{4}$, 4. The lowest number into which both a 3 and a 4 can divide is 12. So 12 is the lowest common denominator.

- The chief rule of equivalence is to do the same to the numerator as you do to the denominator. To get a denominator of 12, we multiplied the denominator 3 in $\frac{1}{3}$ by 4, so must do the same to the numerator 1. Thus, $\frac{1}{3}$ = $\frac{4}{12}$. Meanwhile, in $\frac{1}{4}$ we multiplied the denominator 4 by 3, and must now do the same to the numerator. So $\frac{1}{4}$ = $\frac{3}{12}$. Our sum is now $\frac{4}{12} + \frac{3}{12}$.

- When adding or subtracting vulgar fractions, leave the lowest common denominator as it is and apply the addition or subtraction to the numerators only. 4 + 3 = 7 so the answer is $\frac{7}{12}$.

- Equally, If we were subtracting $\frac{1}{4}$ from $\frac{1}{3}$, the calculation would have been $\frac{4}{12} - \frac{3}{12} = \frac{1}{12}$.

Exercise 22

Solve the following sums, giving your answer in its simplest form.

1) $\frac{4}{9} - \frac{2}{9} = ?$

2) $\frac{3}{7} + \frac{4}{7} = ?$

3) $\frac{2}{5} + \frac{7}{10} = ?$

4) $\frac{3}{4} - \frac{2}{3} = ?$

5) $\frac{3}{7} + \frac{5}{9} = ?$

Little by Little

Multiplying vulgar fractions is nice and simple since you need not concern yourself with equivalence. Simply multiply the numerators together and then do the same with the denominators. So $\frac{1}{3} \times \frac{3}{4} = \frac{3}{12}$ (which can, of course, be simplified to $\frac{1}{4}$).

Should you be multiplying a fraction by a whole number, the whole number can be expressed as $\frac{n}{1}$ (e.g. if the whole number n is 5, it can be written as $\frac{5}{1}$ if it helps you to do your calculation).

You might also be confronted by a mixed number – e.g. one that includes a whole number and a fraction, such as $2\frac{1}{4}$. Adding or subtracting mixed numbers is straightforward enough since you add or subtract the whole numbers first and then do the same with the fractions separately. But if multiplying them together, you must first convert them into top-heavy fractions (also known as improper fractions). To do this, use the denominator in the fraction of the mixed number as the denominator in your top-heavy fraction too. So for $2\frac{1}{4}$, 4 is the denominator. 2 is equal to $\frac{8}{4}$, so to get our top-heavy fraction for $2\frac{1}{4}$ we add $\frac{8}{4} + \frac{1}{4}$ to get $\frac{9}{4}$ in total. Once you have your top-heavy fractions, you can multiply the fractions together as before. Thus, $2\frac{1}{4} \times \frac{3}{5} = \frac{9}{4} \times \frac{3}{5} = \frac{27}{20}$.

Exercise 23

1) Solve the following, putting your results into their simplest form.
   a) $\frac{1}{2} \times \frac{3}{4} = ?$
   b) $2 \times \frac{3}{5} = ?$
   c) $\frac{1}{3} \times \frac{2}{3} \times \frac{6}{7} = ?$

2) Convert the following mixed numbers into top-heavy fractions, and top-heavy fractions into mixed numbers.
   a) $2\frac{4}{7}$
   b) $\frac{27}{5}$
   c) $7\frac{5}{8}$
   d) $\frac{123}{17}$

3) Solve the following, putting your results into their simplest form.
   a) $7\frac{1}{3} \times \frac{3}{4} = ?$
   b) $2\frac{1}{2} \times 3\frac{3}{4} = ?$
   c) $1\frac{1}{2} \times 3\frac{3}{8} \times 2\frac{1}{4} = ?$

The Bare Essentials

The process of *cancelling down* is reliant on the equivalence of fractions and is particularly useful in simplifying particularly difficult multiplication sums. The key thing to remember is that when multiplying vulgar fractions, you can put any numerator on any denominator without affecting the answer. So, for example, $\frac{3}{7}$ x $\frac{2}{5}$ gives the same result as $\frac{2}{7}$ x $\frac{3}{5}$ (namely, $\frac{6}{35}$).

Let's cancel down a more complex sum: $\frac{5}{18}$ x $\frac{9}{13}$.

- While it's simple enough to multiply the numerators (9 x 5), the denominators pose more of a challenge.

- We know that we can rewrite this sum as $\frac{9}{18}$ x $\frac{5}{13}$.

- Through our knowledge of equivalence of fractions, we also know that $\frac{9}{18}$ = $\frac{1}{2}$. So the sum can be written much more simply as $\frac{1}{2}$ x $\frac{5}{13}$.

- This gives us a result of $\frac{5}{26}$. So $\frac{5}{18}$ x $\frac{9}{13}$ = $\frac{5}{26}$.

Exercise 24

Solve the following sums by cancelling down.

1) $\frac{3}{17}$ x $\frac{5}{6}$ = ?
2) $\frac{3}{5}$ x $\frac{4}{27}$ = ?
3) $\frac{4}{5}$ x $\frac{11}{16}$ = ?
4) $\frac{29}{32}$ x $\frac{2}{87}$ = ?

Making a Little Less

Despite what you might think, dividing vulgar fractions is a relatively simple process. Fortunately, you won't need to undertake complex long division-esque calculations because you can get to your answer by multiplying instead. However, before you can do this, you must remember to invert your second fraction (the one you're dividing by). By inverting, we simply mean turn it upside down so the denominator becomes the numerator and vice versa. Here's a worked example using the sum $\frac{2}{8} \div \frac{3}{7}$:

- First, turn the second equation upside down. The sum is thus now $\frac{2}{8} \div \frac{7}{3}$.

- Next, substitute the division symbol for a multiplication sign: $\frac{2}{8} \times \frac{7}{3}$.

- Now, make your calculation: $\frac{2}{8} \times \frac{7}{3} = \frac{14}{24}$.

- Simplify your answer, if possible: $\frac{14}{24} = \frac{7}{12}$.

- Therefore, $\frac{2}{8} \div \frac{3}{7} = \frac{7}{12}$.

Exercise 25

Work out the following sums and give your answer in its simplest form. If your answer is a top-heavy fraction, convert it into a mixed number.

1) $\frac{1}{2} \div \frac{3}{4} = ?$
2) $\frac{2}{3} \div \frac{3}{5} = ?$

3) $\frac{1}{13} \div \frac{1}{13} = ?$
4) $\frac{13}{15} \div \frac{9}{10} = ?$

MAKING THE POINT: DECIMALS

As we've already seen on page 161, in decimal numbers the fraction appears after a decimal point, with each proceeding column possessing a steadily decreasing place value. So, for example, 0.5 (equivalent to $\frac{1}{2}$) is bigger than 0.05 (equivalent to $\frac{1}{20}$).

Give and Take

As we also previously saw, we add or subtract decimals in exactly the same way as whole numbers. If you have unequal numbers of columns, though, it helps to equalize them by adding zeros as necessary. Thus:

7.91 -   becomes   7.910 -
5.447   5.447

Exercise 26

Solve the following sums.

1) $3.85 + 0.67 = ?$
2) $9.674 + 2.28 = ?$
3) $8.47 - 6.85 = ?$
4) $11.2 - 3.657 = ?$

Everything in Its Place

Multiplying with decimals is decidedly easier if you remove the decimal point while you're doing the calculation and put it back in once you have your result. It should be reinserted so that your answer has the same number of decimal places as there were in the original sum. Here are two examples to illustrate the point:

- 12 x 0.6 – remove the decimal point to get 12 x 6.

- 12 x 6 = 72.

- You had 1 decimal place in the original sum so you need 1 decimal place in the answer. Your answer is thus 7.2.

- 4.8 x 6.2 – remove the decimal points to get 48 x 62.

- 48 x 62 = 2,976

- You had 2 decimal places in the original sum so add 2 places to the answer. Your answer is thus 29.76!

Dividing with decimals, meanwhile, is straightforward enough if dividing by a whole number, since we treat it like any other division sum, remembering to insert a decimal point in the correct place. Hence, 18.4 ÷ 4 becomes:

$$4\overline{)\begin{array}{c} 0\ \ 4\ \cdot\ 6 \\ 1\ \ ^18\ \cdot\ ^24 \end{array}} \quad \text{so } 18.4 \div 4 = 4.6$$

However, if you're dividing a decimal by another decimal, you'll once again need to employ your knowledge of equivalence of fractions:

- Firstly, think of the sum as a vulgar fraction. For instance, $16.2 \div 0.6$ would be expressed as $^{16.2}\!/_{0.6}$.

- Next, turn the denominator (0.6 in this case) into a whole number by multiplying it. Some simple arithmetic reveals that we can multiply 0.6 by 5 to get 3.

- Now do to the numerator as you have done to the denominator. Here, we multiplied 0.6 by 5 so must do the same to 16.2. $16.2 \times 5 = 81$.

- The new sum is thus $^{81}\!/_{3}$. This equals 27. So we know that $16.2 \div 0.6$ must also equal 27.

Exercise 27

Now it's time to solve the following.

1) $14 \times 0.6 = ?$
3) $3.8 \times 2.4 = ?$
3) $28.8 \div 0.9 = ?$
4) $4.25 \div 1.7 = ?$

TAKING YOUR CUT: PERCENTAGES

The expression *per cent* derives from the Latin *per centum*, meaning per 100. When using percentages, we're actually expressing a number as a fraction of 100 (with 1 equalling 100%). So, when the likes of Simon Cowell say they believe in something 110%, they're talking nonsense. Percentages often add clarity where a vulgar fraction or a decimal would create confusion. For example, if Boy A gets 68% in his exam and Boy B gets 65%, we have a much clearer idea of their respective score than if we said Boy A got $^{17}\!/_{25}$ and Boy B got $^{13}\!/_{25}$.

Bargain Hunting

However, a percentage is often meaningless if we do not know what it is a percentage of. For example, if we go to buy a car and find out it's for sale that day at 20% off, we're none the wiser as to how much money we'll need if we don't know what it was originally priced at. However, if the car was originally £1,600, we can quickly work out what it costs now:

- Firstly, we calculate 20% of £1,600, which we do by dividing 1,600 by 100 and then multiplying the result by 20.

- 1,600 ÷ 100 x 20 = 320.

- Now we subtract 320 from our original 1,600, to give 1,280.

- The price with 20% off is thus £1,280.

You may also want to calculate a percentage rate. For example, if 17 out of 25 pupils pass an exam, what is the pass percentage rate? The key is to turn your two known figures into a vulgar fraction (in this case $^{17}\!/_{25}$) and multiply both by 100. Try to cancel down the denominator and 100 wherever possible. In this case, the sum $^{17}\!/_{25}$ x 100 cancels down to $^{17}\!/_{1}$ x 4 = 68. The pass rate is thus 68%.

Exercise 28

Use your knowledge of percentages to answer the following questions.

1) A jumper that originally cost £50 is on sale at 20% off. What is its new price?

2) A home cinema originally cost £680 but is on sale at 30% off. What is the value of the reduction?

3) In a survey, 6 out of 10 people reported that they had a credit card. Express this as a percentage.

4) Of 220 people surveyed, 121 had a university degree. What percentage of respondents had a degree?

Highs and Lows

Sometimes it's useful to know how much more or less a new figure is than an old one. For example, imagine your weekly wage increases from £200 to £212. Knowing the value of the weekly wage is important but knowing the percentage increase will provide additional information, such as whether your raise matches or exceeds the rate of inflation.

To calculate a percentage increase:

- Take your initial figure, Value A (£200 in this case) and subtract it from the new figure, Value B (£212). B - A = 212 - 200 = 12.

- Now divide your result by Value A: 12 ÷ 200 = 0.06.

- Multiply the result by 100: 0.06 x 100 = 6.

- Your weekly wage has thus increased by 6%.

This time, imagine that your employer has had to tighten the purse strings and has reduced your weekly wage from £200 to £175. To calculate the percentage decrease:

- Subtract the new figure, Value B (£175) from the original figure, Value A (£200). A - B = 200 - 175 = 25.

- Divide the result by Value A: 25 ÷ 200 = 0.125.

- Multiply that figure by 100: 0.125 x 100 = 12.5.

- Your weekly wage has thus decreased by 12.5%.

Exercise 29

Now calculate the percentage increases and decreases in the following problems.

1) A football club raises its adult ticket price from £48 per to £60. What is the percentage increase in price?

2) A round of half-time refreshments falls in price from £12.50 to £10.25. What is the percentage decrease in price?

3) The number of away fans at the local derby game was 850 one season, but 952 the next. What is the percentage increase season on season?

4) However, the number of home fans at the corresponding games fell from 1,740 to 1,479. What is the percentage decrease season on season?

WHAT ARE THE CHANCES? PROBABILITY

Probability deals with the likelihood of whether certain events will occur or not. There are a few fundamentals to get to grips with in probability theory before we proceed. Firstly, at the most basic level, any given event may be classified as possible or impossible. While it might be highly unlikely that you'll ever holiday on Saturn, it's not impossible. However, dealing five aces from a standard pack of cards is. Events may also be seen in terms of being certain or uncertain, and again you may be surprised at just how few 'sure things' there really are. Rolling a standard dice will give you a number between 1 and 6 – that is certain. As for the sun rising tomorrow – well, likely as it is, it isn't a certainty.

Back to Frac(tions)

Fortunately, not much of the probability theory that we deal with in everyday life requires us to make these sorts of philosophical judgements, though it does you well to be aware of the theory. Most of the time, we calculate probability by dealing with our old friend, vulgar fractions:

- If we flip a coin, it will land either heads or tails up. Therefore, there is a 1 in 2 chance of it coming up heads (or indeed tails), odds that we can represent as $\frac{1}{2}$.

- The odds of rolling a particular number on a standard 6-sided die is $\frac{1}{6}$.

- To calculate the odds of multiple events occurring, we simply multiply together the odds of each individual event. So the chances of flipping a coin and getting a head and then rolling a dice and getting a six is $\frac{1}{2}$ x $\frac{1}{6}$, which equals $\frac{1}{12}$.

- Remember, the odds for some events change the more times you do them. While the odds of a coin landing heads up when you flip it is always 1 in 2, the same cannot be said for drawing an ace from a pack of cards. The odds of doing this with a standard pack of cards is 4 in 52 (the number of cards in a pack) the first time you try. But, assuming you don't replace the drawn card back in the pack, the next time you try you will be picking from only 51 cards, so the odds become 4 in 51 (or 3 in 51 if you drew an ace with your first card).

Exercise 30

Work out the odds for each of the following events or series of events.

1) Getting a heads and then a tails from two consecutive coin flips.
2) Flipping four consecutive heads.
3) Rolling a 5 or 6 three times in a row in consecutive rolls of a standard 6-sided dice.
4) Picking a red card and then a black card consecutively from a standard playing deck of cards.

5) Consecutively picking the Queen of Spades followed
    by any other picture card from a standard playing deck
    of cards.

6) Winning the lottery by correctly matching six numbers
    randomly selected from all the numbers between 1 and 49.
    The numbers can appear in any order and any number can
    be selected only once.

MIDDLE OF THE ROAD: AVERAGES

Averaging is the process of analyzing data to find the single value
that summarizes the data set as a whole. However, any group of
data can have more than one type of average. The three 'averages'
in everyday usage are:

*   *Mean* – the most familiar form of average, calculated by
    adding together the values of each datum in a data set and
    then dividing the result by how many data there are in
    total. So, for example, to find the mean age of 5 people, add
    together each of their ages and divide by 5.

*   *Median* – the middle datum in a data set. If our 5 subjects
    were aged 10, 22, 36, 47 and 92, the median would be
    36 (the third of the five values). Where there is an even
    number of data, the median is the mean of the middle
    two numbers.

*   *Mode* – the value that occurs most frequently in a data
    set. Imagine our subjects' ages were 10, 22, 47, 47 and 92.

47 would be the mode as it appears twice, while the other ages only appear once. It's possible that a data set will have no mode or indeed more than one.

Exercise 31

Below is a data set of the exam results of 12 students, with Pupil A scoring the lowest and Pupil L the highest:

A	B	C	D	E	F	G	H	I	J	K	L
11%	39%	48%	53%	62%	62%	66%	68%	71%	71%	75%	88%

1) What is the mean average of the students' results (to the nearest half a per cent)?
2) What is the median score?
3) What is the mode score?
4) After a re-mark, pupils J, K and L were each given an additional mark. What is the new mode of the data set?

WHEN IS A NUMBER NOT A NUMBER? ALGEBRA

Using letters in place of numbers might seem a bit mad, but, believe me, there's method in the madness. In *algebra*, we use letters in place of certain unknown numbers. We do this when we have an equation or a formula where one or more elements has an unknown value but a fixed relationship with the other values. (And for the record, there are no set rules on which letters should replace which numbers, so feel free to improvise!)

In the first instance, it's worth establishing the difference between a regular equation and a formula (which is a special sort of equation):

- In an *equation*, any letter has only a limited number of possible values (and often only one). For example, in the equation 3 + a = 5, a can only equal 2.

- However, in a *formula*, there can be a whole range of values.
  - For example, the formula for calculating speed (s) involves dividing distance travelled (d) by time taken (t). Or s = d ÷ t. This equation means that as long as we know the distance and the time (whatever values those might be), we have the tools to work out the speed. For example:
    - d = 10 km   t = 0.5 hours
    - s = d ÷ t = 10 ÷ 0.5 = 20 km/hour
  - Equally, d might be 100 km or 5,000 km or 35 metres, and t might be 3 hours or 6 hours or 6 weeks, but we can still calculate s.

When dealing with an algebraic equation, it's useful to be versed in the correct terminology:

- Each side of an equation is called an *expression*.

- Any number or letter is called a *factor*.

- When letters and/or numbers are multiplied together, this is known as a *term* (e.g. 3a). In algebraic terms like this, there's no need for a multiplication sign.

- Within a *term*, there's a *coefficient* (e.g. the 3 in 3a) and a *variable* (e.g. the a in 3a).

- *Like terms* are two or more terms that have the same unknown (or unknowns) with the same power. For example, a^2 and $3a^2$ are like terms, as are a and 3a (in this latter example the unknown, a, has the same power, 1, in each case).

- *Unlike terms* are any terms that don't have the same unknown (or unknowns) with the same power. For example, a and a^2 are unlike terms, as are a and b.

The Basics

With all this information to get to grips with before even embarking on solving an equation, algebra may seem very complicated. In truth, some of it is. However, mastering the basics should be well within your grasp. When confronted by an algebraic problem, keep in mind these two key points:

- The goal is always to isolate a particular unknown on one side of the = sign so as to work out its value using the sum on the other side of the = sign.

- Wherever possible, simplify expressions, always remembering that what you do to one side of an equation you must also do to the other side.

Here's a really simple algebraic conundrum to start us off:

- Three boys – Sam, Geoff and Joe – go fishing. Sam catches three fish. Geoff catches 7 fish. Altogether, the 3 boys catch 16 fish. How many fish did Joe catch?

- We can express this problem using algebra, replacing the unknown quantity (the number of fish caught by Joe) with a letter (let's choose a for simplicity).

- We thus have a sum: $a + 3 + 7 = 16$.

- We can immediately simplify this to $a + 10 = 16$.

- In order to isolate the a, we need to get rid of that 10. To do so, we simply subtract it, giving an expression on the left of $a + 10 - 10$.

- Having done that in the expression on the left, we must also do it on the right. So the equation is now $a + 10 - 10 = 16 - 10$. Or, more simply, $a = 6$.

- So we know that Joe caught 6 fish.

Exercise 32

Solve the following equations, remembering the BIDMAS rules detailed on page 151.

1) $a + 12 = 37$
2) $28 - c = 19$
3) $4d = 28$

4) $2e - 6 = 40$
5) $f/3 - 7 = 12$

Simple Minds

So far, we've looked at very basic algebraic equations. As you encounter more difficult problems, you'll need to employ other methods to simplify them.

- Simplify like terms. Any terms, whether like or unlike, can be multiplied or divided together. But only like terms can be added or subtracted. (e.g. $2a - 7 + a$ can be simplified to $3a - 7$).

- Simplify indices. If you're multiplying unknowns or numbers that are the same, you can combine their indices by adding them together. For example, $2^2 \times 2^3$ is the same as 2^{2+3} or 2^5.

- If there are coefficients attached to the unknowns, add the indices as above and multiply the coefficients. Thus, $5a^2 \times 3a^3$ becomes $(5 \times 3) \times a^{2+3}$, or $15a^5$.

- Dividing with indices works in the opposite way. That's to say, indices are subtracted and coefficients divided. So, for example:
  - $a^5 \div a^3$ is the same as $a^{5-3,}$ or $a^{2.}$ (Note, you can have negative indices!)
  - $16a^5 \div 4a^3$ is the same as $(16 \div 4)\ a^{5-3}$, or $4a^2$.

You'll also find that the unknown sometimes sits within brackets. In such cases, you'll need to deliver the unknown outside of its brackets by doing something known as expanding brackets. To do this, multiply everything inside the brackets by whatever sits immediately outside of them. For example, say your equation is $5(a + 2) = 30$:

- Take $5(a + 2)$ and turn it into $(5 \times a) + (5 \times 2)$.

- This can then be simplified, in this case to $5a + 10$.

- The equation now reads $5a + 10 = 30$. Therefore, $5a = 30 - 10 = 20$.

- If $5a = 20$, $a = {}^{20}/_5 = 4$.

- Remember to keep any operation signs (e.g. +, -) with the figure to their right. Hence, $5(a - 2)$ becomes $(5 \times a) + (5 \times -2)$ and can be further simplified to $5a - 10$.

Some equations have unknowns on both sides of the = sign. If you're confronted by such an equation, you should first seek to balance it so that there are unknowns only on one side. Let's look at the sum $4 + 2a = 3a + 1$:

- To remove the unknown on the left, we can subtract $2a$.

- We must then do the same to the expression on the right. The equation is now $4 = a + 1$.

- To isolate the a on the right, we simply subtract 1, and do the same to the left side. Hence, 4 - 1 = a + 1 - 1. Or to put it more simply, a = 3.

Exercise 33

Using the strategies detailed on the previous page, solve the following problems.

1) $5a - 2a + 3 = 15$
2) $c^4 \div c = 125$
3) $3(d + 5) = 33$
4) $-6(e - 3) = 48$
5) $6f + 5 = 5f + 14$
6) $7g - 23 = 4(g + 4)$

Altogether Now

Simultaneous equations are two equations that are both true at the same time and which contain two or more unknowns to be found. The simplest way to solve them is to add or subtract one from the other to eliminate one of the unknowns from the equation.

- Take the following equations:
  - $2a + b = 12$
  - $3a - b = 13$

- Adding the equations together gives us 5a = 25 (since the +b and –b cancel each other out). So *a* = 25 ÷ 5 = 5.

- To ascertain the value of *b*, we simply put the value of *a* into either equation and discover that b must equal 2.

However, sometimes it's impossible to eliminate either of the unknowns by this method. If this is the case, factor up one of the equations until you can. Look at the following example:

- ○ 4c + 3d = 50
- ○ 2c - d = 10

- Add them together and we get 6c + 2d = 60. Subtract one from the other and we get 2c + 4d = 40. Neither really helps us.

- Instead, we must factor up the second equation as simply as possible so that it can be subtracted from the first one. In this case, by factoring by 2, we get 4c - 2d = 20. The 4c in each equation will now cancel each other out.
  - ○ 4c + 3d = 50
  - ○ 4c - 2d = 20

- A simple subtraction leaves us with 5d = 30. Therefore, d = 30 ÷ 5 = 6. Plug 6 into either equation in place of *d* and we can then calculate that *c* must equal 8.

Exercise 34

Answer the following simultaneous equations, giving figures for both the unknowns in each case.

1) If 5a + 2b = 53 and 3a + 6b = 75, what are the values of a and b?

2) If 6c - d = 13 and 2c + d = 19, what are the values of c and d?

3) Martin buys 3 shirts and a jumper for a total of £131. Ahmed goes to the same store and buys 4 shirts and 2 jumpers for £207. Assuming a standard price for shirts and a standard price for jumpers, how much does a shirt cost and how much for a jumper?

ANSWERS

SECTION I: READING

Answers to Exercise 1

1) A tenor and a contralto.

2) Banjos and traps (percussion instruments).

3) Yellow.

4) Jordan Baker, a man and a 'rowdy little girl'.

Answers to Exercise 2

1) Health, spirits and money.

2) Hampstead.

3) Two nights.

4) Three, of five.

5) Sarah.

Answers to Exercise 3

1) At the back of their house.

2) Flowers and herbs, including rampion (rapunzel).

3) A salad.

4) Three times as much.

5) As much as he wanted.

Answers to Exercise 4

1) In the forest.

2) The speech of the learned.

3) The songs of the woodlands.

4) Because his wings are powerless and dead.

Answers to Exercise 5

1) 10.

2) 27 December 1831.

3) Teneriffe.

4) Cows, goats, kingfishers, grasshoppers and lizards.

Answers to Exercise 6

1) By clasping her baby to herself.

2) It is described as 'haughty'.

3) On the breast of her gown.

4) Deep black.

Answers to Exercise 7

1) The goat, the sheep and the calf.

2) It's easier to enter an enemy's lair than to leave it.

3) The fox is wily. He is far less trusting than the sheep, the goat and the calf. His quiet observation of the lion's methods saves him.

Answers to Exercise 8

1) No. He is described as 'being new to a river and riverside life and its ways'.

2) a) Petulantly, irritably

   b) Rowed a boat

   c) The act of moving an oar through the water.

3) He is presumably older, since he refers to Mole as 'my young friend'.

4) The narrator heightens the comedy of the accident when Rat's slight air of 'other-worldliness' is pricked as he is seen flailing in the bottom of the boat, his heels in the air.

Answers to Exercise 9

1) Jackson, Tennessee.
2) Their knapsacks were large and caused chafing on the shoulders.
3) A rolled-up blanket.
4) The soldiers of foreign birth.
5) a) Rubbed
   b) Increased
   c) Stuffed
   d) Spoils

Answers to Exercise 10

1) Money.
2) A lark flying into the sky at daybreak.
3) The narrator begins by bemoaning his personal circumstances, cursing his fate and feeling hopeless. He is envious of the achievements of others. However, thoughts of his love lift his spirits and by the end of the poem he would not change places even with a king.

Answers to Exercise 11

1) Olive.
2) A chin that juts out. Also known as the Habsburg jaw, which here creates an association between the Emperor and one of the great European ruling families.
3) His sword is described as less than three inches long.
4) a) Appearance, carriage, manner.
   b) Speculated, concluded.
   c) A little, a bit.

Answers to Exercise 12

1) a) Showing good manners.

   b) Exerted themselves.

   c) Shivering in the cold.

2) 'Feels' in the second line of the sixth stanza.

3) In the previous stanzas Emily Dickinson had been reflecting on her own life. She is now old.

Answers to Exercise 13

1) The early part of the night, before the fog has taken grip.

2) Longer ago. It is described that the maid, when narrating the experience, 'used to say' she had never felt more at peace. This suggests that the story has been told often in the past, so the events themselves must be even further in the past.

3) To be close enough to be able to talk to each other.

4) He is described as having a 'very pretty manner of politeness' and as having an 'innocent and old-world kindness of disposition'.

Answers to Exercise 14

1) A doctor's surgery (in fact, the surgery of Dr Watson).

2) No. The guard states that he brought the patient round to the surgery himself so that he 'couldn't slip away'.

3) Bohemian literally means related to Bohemia, now a region within the Czech Republic. However, in this context it relates to a person of unconventional behaviour and manners, often with an interest in the arts.

Answers to Exercise 15

1) a) Making a sorrowful or high-pitched sound.

   b) Throwing corn in a breeze to separate the wheat from the chaff.

   c) Damp, moist.

2) A person who picks up grain in a field after harvesting.

3) By describing the appearance of the robin (traditionally associated with winter) and depicting the gathering of the swallows as they prepare for migration.

Answers to Exercise 16

1) 7 a.m.

2) She was a maid and she was preparing a great feast.

3) A bakery associated with the king located on Pudding Lane.

4) Because he believed it was far enough away not to cause any imminent danger.

Answers to Exercise 17

1) On a riverbank.

2) We are told that the day is hot and that Alice was feeling 'very sleepy'.

3) Anthropomorphism.

Answers to Exercise 18

1) A whaleship.

2) Stupid or foolish.

3) The author is referring to Captain Peleg shouting orders at the men on the boat.

Answers to Exercise 19

1) c) one iota
2) Learning to whistle.
3) His home, St Petersburg, is described as a 'poor little shabby village'. Also, the fact that the new boy is smartly dressed on a weekday is described as 'simply astounding'. Indeed, it is implied that a child wearing shoes on a Friday is a feature of note. Finally, the new boy's finery is contrasted against Tom's own outfit, which seemed to grow 'shabbier and shabbier'.
4) Beat in a fight.

SECTION II: WRITING

Answers to Exercise 1

Column A	Column B	Column C
1) Noun	A 'naming' word for a person, thing or place.	Car, dog, France
2) Verb	A 'doing' word that describes an action or a state of being.	To be, to drive, to swim
3) Pronoun	A word used as a substitute for a noun, usually referring to a participant in the sentence or a noun already mentioned.	You, us, something
4) Adjective	A word that describes a noun.	Beautiful, colourful, broken

5) Adverb	A word that adds meaning to a verb.	Vaguely, avidly, slowly
6) Preposition	A word used before a noun or pronoun to express the relationship between it and another object.	On, behind, during
7) Conjunction	A 'joining' word that links together sentences, phrases or clauses.	Until, and, though
8) Interjection	A 'stand-alone' word that expresses emotion.	Yikes, hurrah, shh

Answers to Exercise 2

1) I enjoy watching <u>football</u>.

2) Jack knew <u>himself</u> very well but didn't trust <u>them</u>.

3) <u>Either</u> we win the lottery <u>or</u> I'll have to go back to work.

4) The pupil had the <u>neatest</u> handwriting in the school.

5) The dog <u>sprinted</u> across the beach.

6) '<u>Good grief!</u>' said the woman as she inspected her new haircut.

7) <u>She</u> despises custard with her apple pie.

8) The sprinter <u>rapidly</u> accelerated.

9) The train chugged <u>through</u> the tunnel.

10) A <u>shimmering</u> diamond sat in the centre of the ring.

11) The injured man screamed <u>piercingly</u>.

12) The nuns ran <u>over</u> the hill.

13) My <u>family</u> went to the <u>theatre</u>.

14) He was talented <u>but</u> lacked application.

15) The doctor <u>concluded</u> his examination.

16) The prima ballerina returned to the stage amid calls of '<u>Encore!</u>'

Answers to Exercise 3

door	noun
upon	preposition
dismal	adjective
for	conjunction
shovel	noun
himself	pronoun
failed	verb
you	pronoun
cried	verb
of	preposition
Bah!	interjection

Answers to Exercise 4

1) Abstract
2) Proper
3) Concrete
4) Concrete
5) Abstract
6) Proper

Answers to Exercise 5

1) Rattlesnake
2) Countryside
3) Greenhouse
4) Pancake
5) Shorthand
6) Hanger-on
7) Swimming pool
8) Check-in
9) Over-ripe
10) Full moon

Answers to Exercise 6

1) Non-countable
2) Countable

3) Non-countable

4) Countable

5) Countable

Answers to Exercise 7

1) He rushed his work and would have benefited from **less** haste.

2) She had **a couple of** tickets for the gigs so asked her best friend along.

3) **Too few** people take exercise.

4) Though **a lot of** the tapestry was destroyed, **a**

little remained in perfect condition.

5) **Too much** chocolate is bad for you.

6) The friends went for **a few** drinks.

7) **Too many** rugby players get injured.

8) For a diplomat, he had **a lack of** tact.

Answers to Exercise 8

1) Do you have **any** playing cards at home?

2) Would **somebody** like to help me out?

3) She didn't know **anybody** at her new school.

4) Do you know **anyone** who

can give us a lift?

5) You know **something** about this, don't you?

6) I couldn't sleep after I had **some** coffee.

7) Is there **any** coffee in the pot?

Answers to Exercise 9

1) French fries

2) Days

3) Taxes

4) Potatoes

5) Hoofs or hooves
6) Quizzes
7) Fish or fishes
8) Wives

Answers to Exercise 10

1) Children
2) Mice
3) Sheep
4) Teeth
5) Oxen
6) Stadia
7) Stimuli
8) Crises
9) Women
10) Indices
11) Media
12) Species

Answers to Exercise 11

1) Most of the crew **were** killed in the crash.
2) The crew **was** the most respected in the company.
3) The audience **is** singing along with the chorus.
4) Some of the audience **are** demanding refunds.
5) The interview panel **was** interrogating the candidate.
6) The interview panel **were** not in agreement about whom to appoint.

Answers to Exercise 12

1) She is going to buy **a** hat for the wedding.
2) He looks ridiculous in **the** hat his wife bought him.
3) The Taj Mahal is **a** beautiful building.
4) The Taj Mahal is **the** best-known site in India.
5) Do you have **an** idea of the price?
6) Do you know the price of **a** loaf of bread?

Answers to Exercise 13

1) Anna could not believe **her** luck.

2) After scoring the winning goal, the team ran to the corner and celebrated with **one other**.

3) Did you do that to **yourself**?

4) Fred and Joe were best friends and spent all their time playing with **each other**.

5) We bought **ourselves** a new car.

6) If I had found the treasure it would be **mine** but they found **it** so it's **theirs**.

Answers to Exercise 14

1) The breaded chicken, **which** was filled with garlic butter, was over cooked.

2) He **who** lives in a glass house should not throw stones.

3) I was invited to a party for my neighbour **who's** about to turn ninety.

4) The judges gave a prize to the person **whose** marrow was largest.

5) The beach **that** we visited was beautiful.

6) **Whom** did he decide to invite to the show?

Answers to Exercise 15

1) **Whose** palace is this?

2) To **whom** should I address this letter?

3) **Who** wrote *Oliver Twist*?

4) **What** are you carrying?

5) **Which** sprinter do you think will win the race?

Answers to Exercise 16

1) **No one** can turn back the clock.

2) I must buy her **something** for her birthday.

3) I want **that** one over there.

4) Are **these** on the table here all for me?

5) Do you know **someone** who can fix my car who won't charge too much?

6) I only meant to eat one cake but ended up having **several**.

7) I can't choose just one because I love them **all**.

8) Were **those** your friends at the party last night?

Answers to Exercise 17

	To be	To have	To do	To go
	Present	**Present**	**Present**	**Present**
I	am	have	do	go
You	are	have	do	go
He/she/it	is	has	does	goes
We	are	have	do	go
You	are	have	do	go
They	are	have	do	go

	Past	**Past**	**Past**	**Past**
I	was	had	did	went
You	were	had	did	went
He/she/it	was	had	did	went
We	were	had	did	went
You	were	had	did	went

Present participle	being	having	doing	going
Past participle	been	had	done	gone

Answers to Exercise 18

Infinitive	Past simple	Past participle
To arise	arose	arisen
To bear	bore	born/borne
To become	became	become
To blow	blew	blown
To burst	burst	burst
To buy	bought	bought
To catch	caught	caught
To choose	chose	chosen
To cut	cut	cut
To do	did	done
To draw	drew	drawn
To drive	drove	driven
To eat	ate	eaten
To fall	fell	fallen
To fly	flew	flown
To forget	forgot	forgotten
To give	gave	given
To grow	grew	grown
To hide	hid	hidden

To keep	kept	kept
To lie	lay	lain
To mistake	mistook	mistaken
To read	read	read
To ring	rang	rung
To see	saw	seen
To shake	shook	shaken
To speak	spoke	spoken
To swell	swelled	swollen
To take	took	taken
To tear	tore	torn
To throw	threw	thrown
To write	wrote	written

Answers to Exercise 19

1) Subject: Shakespeare; object: plays

2) Subject: I; object: correspondence

3) Subject: window cleaner; object: round

4) Subject: window cleaner's wife; object: accounts

5) Subject: driver; object: bus

Answers to Exercise 20

1) Her

2) The soldier

3) His team

4) His audience

Answers to Exercise 21

1) The race was won by the grey horse.

2) That Porsche is owned by the banker.

3) The dentist was visited by the old lady.

4) The king and his family inhabit the palace.

5) The crowd chased the film star down the street,

6) Thomas Hardy wrote *Far From the Madding Crowd.*

Answers to Exercise 22

1) The policeman is chasing a thief.

2) We drove to the nearest hospital.

3) I will have made dinner by the time you get home.

4) They were fishing on the banks of the Ganges.

5) He eats fish and chips every Friday.

6) The tower will have been standing for four centuries next month.

7) They have been studying the Greek myths.

8) You used to visit your Grandma every weekend.

9) He had lost all his money at the casino.

10) I will buy you a car if you pass your exams.

11) He has invested all his money in gold.

12) They will be running the company by this time next year.

Answers to Exercise 23

1) 'You **shall** follow the rules,' warned the referee sternly.

2) Rio **will** host the Olympics in 2016.

3) They announced they **shall** be moving offices.

4) They **will** pay for this!

5) **Will** we ever get out of this traffic jam?

6) **Shall** I get you a gift for your birthday?

Answers to Exercise 24

1) I **ought to** go to the opticians.

2) The Queen **has** visited most of the world's countries.

3) He **would** kill to get tickets for the final.

4) You **couldn't have** made it up.

5) They **do** sing beautifully.

6) She **can't** say we **didn't** try.

Answers to Exercise 25

1) Indicative
2) Imperative
3) Subjunctive
4) Imperative
5) Subjunctive

Answers to Exercise 26

1) Third conditional
2) Zero conditional
3) Second conditional
4) First conditional
5) Second conditional

Answers to Exercise 27

1) The weather is not good today.

2) I would not like to teach the world to sing.

3) I do not always pay my taxes on time.

4) My neighbours do not keep themselves to themselves.

5) The student turned over the exam paper, not panicking.

6) It is tempting not to go.

7) I don't know anything.

8) There's not anyone (or no one) who deserves this more than you.

9) I wasn't anywhere near the crime scene.

Answers to Exercise 28

1) a) Should we not visit?
   b) Shouldn't we visit?
2) a) Could you not try asking?
   b) Couldn't you try asking?
3) a) Have you not eaten enough?
   b) Haven't you eaten enough?
4) a) Are you not the prettiest of them all?
   b) Aren't you the prettiest of them all?
5) a) Shall we not go out tonight?
   b) Shan't we go out tonight?

Answers to Exercise 29

1) **Sensing** the tourists were lost, the man offered directions. (present participle)
2) **Driving** in Italy can be a stressful activity. (gerund)
3) **Touched** by their generosity, he opened the present with a tear in his eye. (past participle)
4) By **speculating** astutely, the stock broker made a fortune. (present participle)
5) **Reading** the newspaper report, the full horror of the situation struck her. (present participle)
6) **Giving** to charity filled Mr Scrooge with a warm glow. (gerund)
7) He tucked into the feast made with ingredients **bought** from the local market. (past participle)
8) The ballerina spun across the stage, **enchanting** the audience. (present participle)
9) She dreamed of **dancing** for the Bolshoi Ballet. (gerund)

Answers to Exercise 30

1) a) Do you have a car?

b) My favourite authors are Dickens, Hardy and Waugh.

c) A pessimist sees the difficulty in every opportunity; an optimist sees the opportunity in every difficulty.

d) She wanted three things from the shop: eggs, bread and butter.

e) Go away! You are not welcome!

2) a) Incorrect. There should be an apostrophe in the contracted 'mustn't'.

b) Correct.

c) Incorrect. Here, 'its' is a possessive pronoun so doesn't need an apostrophe.

d) Incorrect. Where words end in an -iz or -eeze sound (such as Sophocles), we don't add the final 's' if by doing so the word becomes too much of a mouthful.

e) Incorrect. The players are plural so the apostrophe should go after, not before, the 's'.

f) Incorrect. In the case of two or more individuals jointly possessing something, an 's' is needed after the last name only. Hence, we talk of 'Fred and Ginger's movies'.

3) a) Having just left the salon, I felt like a film star!

b) In November 1918, the First World War finally came to an end.

c) Picasso, the famous artist, came from Spain.

d) His favourite films were *The Godfather*, *Rocky* and *Sleepless in Seattle*.

e) The house had been abandoned, its windows smashed.

4) a) 'I'm rich!' he screamed. 'I've won the lottery.'

b) The witness told the judge, 'I heard the defendant demand "Open the safe."'

c) He said he'd be home in twenty minutes.

5) a) He works on the thirty-second floor. It was a forty-four-floor office block.

b) We went on holiday for two weeks. It was the first two-week holiday we'd had in years.

c) He writes with his right hand. He is right-handed.

Answers to Exercise 31

1) Blue (adjective)
2) Awesome (adjective)
3) Triumphantly (adverb)
4) Pre-Columbian (adjective)
5) Fast (adjective)
6) Big (adjective), fast (adverb)
7) Upset (adjective), furiously (adverb)
8) Greatest (adjective), Victorian (adjective)

Answers to Exercise 32

1) Ebenezer Scrooge was tight with his money but my Uncle Fred is <u>meaner</u>.

2) Diamonds are a girl's <u>best</u> friend.

3) After she bit all the girls in her class, Nasty Nancy was the <u>least popular</u> girl in her class.

4) The first comedian was amusing but the second one was <u>funnier</u>.

5) That zombie kung-fu rom-com was the <u>worst</u> film I have ever seen.

6) Many foxes live in the city but badgers are <u>less common</u>.

7) My dog doesn't mind running around our garden but when he's running on the beach he is <u>happier</u>.

8) China is the <u>most populous</u> country in the world.

Answers to Exercise 33

1) He was kept in intensive care because he was **dreadfully** ill with malaria.

2) After three weeks of snow, it was still **bitterly** cold outside.

3) She is an **exceptionally** talented actor.

4) The movie was not great but was **moderately** diverting.

Answers to Exercise 34

1) + f) She arrived at the office early, making herself as busy as a bee.

2) + d) The widower was lost in a sea of grief.

3) + a) He overcame his foe with steely

determination.

4) + h) He approached the situation like a bull in a china shop.

5) + b) The boxer was as hard as nails.

6) + g) He strutted around in his new suit, as proud as a peacock.

7) + c) It was raining cats and dogs.

8) + e) The rumours planted seeds of doubt in her mind.

Answers to Exercise 35

1) He was both a talented singer **and** an adept composer.

2) He phoned the talking clock **so that** he would know the exact time.

3) She might have been old **but** she wasn't very wise.

4) **Neither** Romeo **nor** Juliet lived a long life.

5) He was given a bravery award **because** he helped to catch a thief.

6) He ordered from the menu **as soon as** he arrived at the restaurant.

7) He **not only** bought all the ingredients **but also** baked the cake.

Answers to Exercise 36

1) I have not had a party **since** I was 21.

2) Will you sit in the seat **behind** me?

3) I am available every day **except** Tuesday.

4) The skiers drove off **towards** the mountains.

5) They were picnicking **beneath** the branches of a shady tree.

6) Can you give me a call

after 7 p.m.

7) I could not spot her **among** the crowd of faces.

8) We will be on holiday **from** June **until** July.

9) The cat came in **through** the cat-flap.

10) Meet me in the pub **opposite** the park.

Answers to Exercise 37

1) a) Complex
   b) Complex
   c) Compound

2) a) Restrictive
   b) Non-restrictive
   c) Non-restrictive

3) a) Prepositional phrase
   b) Noun phrase
   c) Verb phrase
   d) Adjectival phrase
   e) Adverbial phrase

Answers to Exercise 38

1) Sitting on the train, Fred was engrossed in the book.

2) Wearing slippers, he drove a bus.

3) Dave often goes back to the hospital where he was born.

4) He was fined for selling tomatoes that had started to rot to customers.

Answers to Exercise 39

1) a) Unpopular
   b) Counter-clockwise
   c) Apolitical
   d) Post-match (or pre-match)
   e) Disreputable
   f) Extra-curricular

2) a) Teacher
   b) Graciousness

c) Mastery
d) Collection
e) Concealment

3) a) National

b) Friendly
c) Fanciful
d) Legendary
e) Debatable

Answers to Exercise 40

1) Free gift
2) Stupid idiot
3) Very unique
4) A variety of different
5) Honest truth

Answers to Exercise 41

1) B
2) B
3) A
4) B
5) B
6) A
7) A
8) B
9) A
10) B
11) A
12) B
13) B
14) A
15) A
16) B
17) B
18) A
19) A
20) B
21) A

Answers to Exercise 42

1) a) The more you practise, the better you'll get.

b) The doctor ran his own practice.

2) a) The trick was ruined

when the audience member said aloud the card he was thinking of.

b) No dogs are allowed on the beach.

3) a) A pail is useful for collecting water.

b) When he saw the price of the meal, he went quite pale.

4) a) The general surveyed his troops, spread out across the plain.

b) When she flies, she likes to sit in the front part of the plane.

5) a) Do you know the people over there?

b) Do you know if their friends are also coming?

6) a) I like all vegetables except celery.

b) I was nervous to join a new team but the other players seemed to accept me.

7) a) Make sure your wedding ring is not too loose.

b) You wouldn't want to lose it.

8) a) The traffic was stationary on the motorway.

b) A prodigious letter-writer, he always bought good stationery.

9) a) The training classes had no effect on the naughty dog.

b) Did the sad film affect you at all?

SECTION III: ARITHMETIC

Answers to Exercise 1

1) 15

2) 73

3) 17

4) 38

Answers to Exercise 2

1) 5

2) 19

3) 37

4) 46

Answers to Exercise 3

1) 48

2) 126

3) 7

4) 22

Answers to Exercise 4

1) 4

2) 5

3) 108

4) 13

Answers to Exercise 5

5	+	8	–	2	**11**
x		x		–	
6	÷	3	x	9	**18**
–		–		+	
7	–	1	x	4	**24**
23		**23**		**-3**	

Answers to Exercise 6

1)	10.47	4)	90 km/hour
2)	22 pence	5)	£2.60
3)	100 miles	6)	14 gallons

Answers to Exercise 7

1)	2	6)	-3
2)	-8	7)	-2
3)	6	8)	7
4)	-6	9)	-19
5)	-11	10)	3

Answers to Exercise 8

1)	-20	5)	7
2)	48	6)	-192
3)	-5	7)	-12
4)	-68	8)	289

Answers to Exercise 9

1)	£154	4)	4,975
2)	£194	5)	£54.79
3)	2,346 pupils	6)	£2,101.44

Answers to Exercise 10

1) a) 162
   b) 513
   c) 3,920

2) a) 4,704
    b) 16,121
    c) 22,581

3) a) 629 hours
    b) 18,415 pupils
    c) 624,747 minutes

Answers to Exercise 11

1) a) 27
    b) 11
    c) 10.5

    c) 13.5

3) a) £18
    b) 11,525
    c) £1,248.50

2) a) 13
    b) 22

Answers to Exercise 12

1) 18
2) 21
3) 72

4) 225
5) 72

Answers to Exercise 13

1) $10 + (36 \div 6) = 16$
2) $16 - (22 + 5) = -11$

3) $108 \div (3 \times 4) + 16 = 25$
4) $(6 \times 22) + (35 \div 5) = 139$

Answers to Exercise 14

1) 16
2) 27
3) 125
4) 36
5) 216

6) 289
7) 8,000

Answers to Exercise 15

1) 8
2) 16
3) 4

4) 14
5) 1,000
6) 25

Answers to Exercise 16

1) 3:2
2) 224
3) 11,200

4) £212.50
5) 20 ml

Answers to Exercise 17

1) 1, 3
2) 1, 2, 3, 4, 6, 12
3) 1, 5, 25

4) 1, 2, 4, 8, 16
5) 1, 2, 3, 4, 6, 8, 9, 12, 18, 24, 36, 72

Answers to Exercise 18

1) a) 23
   b) 113
   c) 251
   d) 757

2) a) 41
   b) 101
   c) 443
   d) 853

Answers to Exercise 19

1) a) 5
   b) 11
   c) 17
   d) 42

2) a) 0.25

   b) 2.75
   c) 1.625

3) a) 111
   b) 1101
   c) 1110

d)   1111101

Answers to Exercise 20

1) a) 10000   2) a) 65
    b) 10011   b) 2.25
    c) 110000   c) 18

Answers to Exercise 21

1) a) $\frac{3}{4}$ 2) a) $\frac{2}{3}$
    b) $\frac{1}{3}$ b) $\frac{5}{8}$
    c) $\frac{5}{6}$ c) $\frac{3}{8}$
    d) $\frac{7}{10}$ d) $\frac{4}{5}$

Answers to Exercise 22

1) $\frac{2}{9}$ 4) $\frac{1}{12}$
2) 1   5) $\frac{62}{63}$
3) $1\frac{1}{10}$

Answers to Exercise 23

1) a) $\frac{3}{8}$
    b) $1\frac{1}{5}$ 3) a) $5\frac{1}{2}$
    c) $\frac{4}{21}$ b) $9\frac{3}{8}$
                          c) $\frac{3}{2} \times \frac{27}{8} \times \frac{9}{4} =$
2) a) $\frac{18}{7}$ $11\frac{25}{64}$
    b) $5\frac{2}{5}$
    c) $\frac{61}{8}$
    d) $7\frac{4}{17}$

Answers to Exercise 24

1) $5/34$

3) $11/20$

2) $4/45$

4) $1/48$

Answers to Exercise 25

1) $2/3$

3) 1

2) $1\frac{1}{9}$

4) $26/27$

Answers to Exercise 26

1) 4.52

3) 1.62

2) 11.954

4) 7.543

Answers to Exercise 27

1) 8.4

3) 32

2) 9.12

4) 2.5

Answers to Exercise 28

1) £40

3) 60%

2) £204

4) 55%

Answers to Exercise 29

1) 25%

3) 12%

2) 18%

4) 15%

Answers to Exercise 30

1) $1/4$

3) $1/27$

2) $1/16$

4) $13/51$

5) $11/_{2,652}$

6) $1/_{13,983,816}$

Answers to Exercise 31

1) 59.5%

2) 64%

3) 62% and 71%

4) 62%

Answers to Exercise 32

1) $a = 25$

2) $c = 9$

3) $d = 7$

4) $e = 23$

5) $f = 57$

Answers to Exercise 33

1) $a = 4$

2) $c = 5$

3) $d = 6$

4) $e = -5$

5) $f = 9$

6) $g = 13$

Answers to Exercise 34

1) $a = 7; b = 9$

2) $c = 4 ; d = 11$

3) Shirt = £27.50; jumper = £48.50

INDEX